g

QUANTITATIVE COMPARISONS & DATA INTERPRETATION

GRE Math Preparation Guide

This volume focuses on two of the GRE's unique quantitative question types. The guide to Quantitative Comparisons briefs students on how to attack these problems and provides time-saving strategies. The guide to Data Interpretation demonstrates approaches to quickly synthesize graphical information on test day.

Quantitative Comparisons/Data Interpretation GRE Preparation Guide, Second Edition

10-digit International Standard Book Number: 1-935707-51-5
13-digit International Standard Book Number: 978-1-935707-51-6
eISBN: 978-1-935707-14-1

Note: *GRE, Graduate Record Examination, Educational Testing Services,* and
ETS are all registered trademarks of Educational Testing Services, which neither
sponsors nor is affiliated in any way with this product.

8 GUIDE INSTRUCTIONAL SERIES

Math GRE Preparation Guides

Algebra
(ISBN: 978-1-935707-47-9)

Fractions, Decimals, & Percents
(ISBN: 978-1-935707-48-6)

Geometry
(ISBN: 978-1-935707-49-3)

Number Properties
(ISBN: 978-1-935707-50-9)

Word Problems
(ISBN: 978-1-935707-54-7)

Quantitative Comparisons & Data Interpretation
(ISBN: 978-1-935707-51-6)

Verbal GRE Preparation Guides

Reading Comprehension & Essays
(ISBN: 978-1-935707-52-3)

Text Completion & Sentence Equivalence
(ISBN: 978-1-935707-53-0)

Manhattan GRE

March 15th, 2011

Dear Student,

Thank you for picking up one of the Manhattan GRE Strategy Guides—we hope that it ends up being just what you need to prepare for the new GRE.

As with most accomplishments, there were many people involved in the book that you're holding. First and foremost is Zeke Vanderhoek, the founder of MG Prep. Zeke was a lone tutor in New York when he started the Company in 2000. Now, ten years later, the Company has Instructors and offices nationwide and contributes to the studies and successes of thousands of students each year.

Our Manhattan GRE Strategy Guides are based on the continuing experiences of our Instructors and our students. On the Company side, we are indebted to many of our Instructors, including but not limited to Roman Altshuler, Chris Berman, Jen Dziura, Dmitry Farber, Stacey Koprince, David Mahler, Seb Moosapoor, Stephanie Moyerman, Chris Ryan, Michael Schwartz, Tate Shafer, Emily Sledge, Tommy Wallach, and Ryan Wessel, all of whom either wrote or edited the books to their present form. Dan McNaney and Cathy Huang provided their formatting expertise to make the books as user-friendly as possible. Last, many people, too numerous to list here but no less appreciated, assisted in the development of the online resources that accompany this guide.

At Manhattan GRE, we continually aspire to provide the best Instructors and resources possible. We hope that you'll find our dedication manifest in this book. If you have any comments or questions, please e-mail me at dan@ manhattangre.com. I'll be sure that your comments reach our curriculum team—and I'll read them too.

Best of luck in preparing for the GRE!

Sincerely,

Dan Gonzalez
Managing Director
Manhattan GRE

www.manhattangre.com   138 West 25th St., 7th Floor   NY, NY 10001   Tel: 646-254-6479   Fax: 646-514-7425

HOW TO ACCESS YOUR ONLINE STUDENT CENTER

If you...

▶ **are a registered Manhattan GRE student**

and have received this book as part of your course materials, you have AUTOMATIC access to ALL of our online resources. To access these resources, follow the instructions in the Welcome Guide provided to you at the start of your program. Do NOT follow the instructions below.

▶ **purchased this book from the Manhattan GRE Online store or at one of our Centers**

1. Go to: http://www.manhattangre.com/studentcenter.cfm

2. Log in using the username and password used when your account was set up. Your one year of online access begins on the day that you purchase the book from the Manhattan GRE online store or at one of our centers.

▶ **purchased this book at a retail location**

1. Go to: http://www.manhattangre.com/access.cfm

2. Log in or create an account.

3. Follow the instructions on the screen.

Your one year of online access begins on the day that you register your book at the above URL.

You only need to register your product ONCE at the above URL. To use your online resources any time AFTER you have completed the registration process, login to the following URL: http://www.manhattangre.com/studentcenter.cfm

Please note that online access is non-transferable. This means that only NEW and UNREGISTERED copies of the book will grant you online access. Previously used books will not provide any online resources.

▶ **purchased an e-book version of this book**

1. Create an account with Manhattan GRE at the website: https://www.manhattangre.com/createaccount.cfm

2. Email a copy of your purchase receipt to books@manhattangre.com to activate your resources. Please be sure to use the same email address to create an account that you used to purchase the e-book.

For any technical issues, email books@manhattangre.com or call 646-254-6479.

TABLE OF CONTENTS

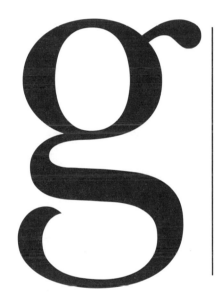

Chapter 1
of

QUANTITATIVE COMPARISONS &
DATA INTERPRETATION

INTRODUCTION &
THE REVISED GRE

In This Chapter . . .

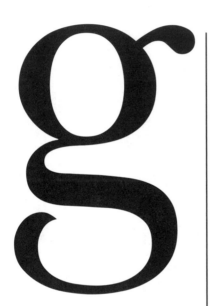

- Introduction, and How to Use Manhattan GRE's Strategy Guides

- The Revised GRE

- Question Formats in Detail

Introduction, and How to Use Manhattan GRE's Strategy Guides

We know that you're looking to succeed on the GRE so that you can go to graduate school and do the things you want to do in life.

We also know that you might not have done math since high school, and that you may never have learned words like "adumbrate" or "sangfroid." We know that it's going to take hard work on your part to get a top GRE score, and that's why we've put together the only set of books that will take you from the basics all the way up to the material you need to master for a near-perfect score, or whatever your score goal may be. You've taken the first step. Now it's time to get to work!

How to Use These Materials

Manhattan GRE's materials are comprehensive. But keep in mind that, depending on your score goal, it may not be necessary to "get" absolutely everything. Grad schools only see your overall Quantitative, Verbal, and Writing scores—they don't see exactly which strengths and weaknesses went into creating those scores.

You may be enrolled in one of our courses, in which case you already have a syllabus telling you in what order you should approach the books. But if you bought this book online or at a bookstore, feel free to approach the books—and even the chapters within the books—in whatever order works best for you. *For the most part, the books, and the chapters within them, are independent; you don't have to master one section before moving on to the next.* So if you're having a hard time with something in particular, you can make a note to come back to it later and move on to another section. Similarly, it may not be necessary to solve every single practice problem for every section. As you go through the material, continually assess whether you understand and can apply the principles in each individual section and chapter. The best way to do this is to solve the Check Your Skills and Practice Problems throughout. If you're confident you have a concept or method down, feel free to move on. If you struggle with something, make note of it for further review. Stay active in your learning and oriented toward the test—it's easy to read something and think you understand it, only to have trouble applying it in the 1–2 minutes you have to solve a problem.

Study Skills

As you're studying for the GRE, try to integrate your learning into your everyday life. For example, vocabulary is a big part of the GRE, as well as something you just can't "cram" for—you're going to want to do at least a little bit of vocab every day. So, try to learn and internalize a little bit at a time, switching up topics often to help keep things interesting.

Keep in mind that, while many of your study materials are on paper (including ETS's most recent source of official GRE questions, *The Official Guide to the GRE revised General Test*), your exam will be administered on a computer. Because this is a computer-based test, you will NOT be able to underline portions of reading passages, write on diagrams of geometry figures, or otherwise physically mark up problems. So get used to this now. Solve the problems in these books on scratch paper. (Each of our books talks specifically about what to write down for different problem types).

Again, as you study stay focused on the test-day experience. As you progress, work on timed drills and sets of questions. Eventually, you should be taking full practice tests (available at www.manhattangre.com) under actual timed conditions.

The Revised GRE

As of August 1, 2011, the Quantitative and Verbal sections of the GRE will undergo a number of changes. The actual body of knowledge being tested won't change, but the *way* it is tested will. Here's a brief summary of what to expect, followed by a more comprehensive assessment of the new exam.

Overall, the general format of the test will change. The length of the test will increase from about 3.5 hours to about 4 hours. There will be two scored math sections and two scored verbal sections rather than one of each, and a new score scale of 130–170 will be used in place of the old 200–800 scale. More on this later.

The Verbal section of the GRE will change dramatically. The Analogies and Antonym questions will disappear. The Sentence Completions and Reading Comprehension will remain, to be expanded and remixed in a few new ways. Vocabulary will still be important, but only in the context of complete sentences. That is, you'll no longer have to worry about vocabulary words standing alone. So for those who dislike learning vocabulary words, the changes will provide partial relief. For those who were looking forward to getting lots of points just for memorizing words, the Manhattan GRE verbal strategy guides will prepare you for the shift.

The Quant section of the GRE prior to August 1, 2011 is composed of multiple choice problems, Quantitative Comparisons, and Data Interpretation questions (which are really a subset of multiple choice problems). The revised test will contain two new problem formats in addition to the current problem formats. However, the type of math, and the difficulty of the math, will remain unchanged.

Additionally, a small four-function calculator with a square root button will appear on-screen. Many test takers will rejoice at the advent of this calculator! It is true that the GRE calculator will reduce emphasis on computation—but look out for problems, such as percents questions with tricky wording, that are likely to foil those who rely on the calculator too much. *In short, the calculator may make your life a bit easier from time to time, but you will never <u>need</u> the calculator to solve a problem.*

Finally, don't worry about whether these new problem types are "harder" or "easier." You are being judged against other test takers, all of whom are in the same boat. So if the new formats are harder, they are harder for other test takers as well.

Exam Structure

The revised test has six sections. You will get a ten-minute break between the third and fourth sections and a one-minute break between the others. The Analytical Writing section is always first. The other five sections can be seen in any order and will include:

- Two Verbal Reasoning sections (approximately 20 questions each in exactly 30 minutes per section)

- Two Quantitative Reasoning sections (approximately 20 questions each in exactly 35 minutes per section)

- Either an "unscored" section or a "research" section

An unscored section will look just like a third Verbal or Quantitative Reasoning section, and you will <u>not</u> be told which of them doesn't count. If you get a research section, it will be identified as such.

Section Type	# Questions	Time	Scored?
Analytical Writing	2 essays	30 minutes each	Yes
Verbal #1	Approx. 20	30 minutes	Yes
Quantitative #1	Approx. 20	35 minutes	Yes
Verbal #2	Approx. 20	30 minutes	Yes
Quantitative #2	Approx. 20	35 minutes	Yes
Unscored Section (verbal or quant)	Approx. 20	30 or 35 min	No
Research Section	Varies	Varies	No

 10 min break

order varies

one or the other, but not both

Later in the chapter, we'll look at all the question formats in detail.

Using the Calculator

The addition of a small, four-function calculator with a square root button means that those taking the revised test can forget re-memorizing their times tables or square roots. However, the calculator is not a cure-all; in many problems, the difficulty is in figuring out what numbers to put into the calculator in the first place. In some cases, using a calculator will actually be less helpful than doing the problem some other way. Let's look at an example:

If x is the remainder when (11)(7) is divided by 4 and y is the remainder when (14)(6) is divided by 13, what is the value of $x + y$?

Solution: This problem is designed so that the calculator won't tell the whole story. Certainly the calculator will tell us that $11 \times 7 = 77$. When you divide 77 by 4, however, the calculator yields an answer of 19.25. The remainder is *not* 0.25 (a remainder is always a whole number).

You might just go back to your pencil and paper, and find the largest multiple of 4 that is less than 77. Since 4 DOES go into 76, we can conclude that 4 would leave a remainder of 1 when dividing into 77. (Notice that we don't even need to know how many times 4 goes into 76, just that it goes in. One way to mentally "jump" to 76 is to say, *4 goes into 40, so it goes into 80 … that's a bit too big, so take away 4 to get 76.*) You could also multiply the leftover 0.25 times 4 (the divisor) to find the remainder of 1.

However, it is also possible to use the calculator to find a remainder. Divide 77 by 4 to get 19.25. Thus, 4 goes into 77 nineteen times, with a remainder left over. Now use your calculator to multiply 19 (JUST 19, not 19.25) by 4. You will get 76. The remainder is $77 - 76 = 1$. Therefore, $x = 1$.

Use the same technique to find y. Multiply 14×6 to get 84. Divide 84 by 13 to get 6.46… Ignore everything after the decimal, and just multiply 6 by 13 to get 78. The remainder is therefore $84 - 78 = 6$. Therefore, $y = 6$.

Since we are looking for $x + y$ and $1 + 6 = 7$, the answer is 7.

You can see that blind faith in the calculator can be dangerous. Use it responsibly! And this leads us to…

Practice Using the Calculator!

On the new GRE, the on-screen calculator will slow you down or lead to incorrect answers if you're not careful! If you plan to use the thing on test day (which you should), you'll want to pactice first.

We have created an online practice calculator for your use. To access this calculator, go to www.manhattangre.com and sign in to the student center using the instructions on the "How to Access Your Online Student Center" page found at the front of this book.

In addition to the calculator, you will see instructions for how to use the calculator. Be sure to read these

instructions and work through the associated exercises. Throughout our math books, you will see the

symbol. This symbol means "use the calculator here!" As much as possible, have the online practice calculator up

and running during your review of our math books. You'll have the chance to use the on-screen calculator when

you take our practice exams as well.

Navigating the Questions in a Section

Another change for test takers on the new GRE is the ability to move freely around the questions in a section… you can go forward and backward one-by-one and can even jump directly to any question from the "review list." The review list provides a snapshot of which questions you have answered, which ones you have tagged for "mark and review," and which are incomplete, either because you didn't select enough answers or because you selected too many (that is, if a number of choices is specified by the question). You should double-check the review list for completion if you finish the section early. Using the review list feature will take some practice as well, which is why we've built it into our online practice exams. Here's some introductory advice.

The majority of test takers will be pressed for time. Thus, for most of you, it won't be feasible to "go back to" multiple problems at the end of the section. Generally, if you can't get a question the first time, you won't be able to get it the second time around either. With this in mind, here's how we recommend using the new review list feature.

1. Do the questions in order as they appear.

2. When you encounter a difficult question, do you best to eliminate answer choices you know are wrong.

3. If you're not sure of an answer, take an educated guess from the choices remaining. Do <u>NOT</u> skip it and hope to return to it later.

4. Using the "mark" button at the top of the screen, mark up to three questions per section that you think you might be able to solve with more time. Mark a question only after you have taken an educated guess.

5. If you have time at the end of the section, click on the review list, identify any questions you've marked and return to them. If you do not have any time remaining, you will have already taken good guesses at the tough ones.

What you want to avoid is "surfing"—clicking forward and backward through the questions searching for the easy ones. This will eat up valuable time. Of course, you'll want to move through the tough ones quickly if you can't get them, but try to avoid skipping stuff.

Again, all of this will take practice. Use our practice exams to fine-tune your approach.

Scoring

Two things have changed about the scoring of the Verbal Reasoning and Quantitative Reasoning sections: (1) how individual questions influence the score and (2) the score scale itself.

For both the Verbal Reasoning and Quantitative Reasoning sections, you will receive a raw score, which is simply how many questions you answered correctly. Your raw score is converted to a scaled score, accounting for the difficulties of the specific questions you actually saw.

The old GRE general section was question-adaptive, meaning that your answer to each question (right or wrong) determined, at least somewhat, the questions that followed (harder or easier). Because you had to commit to an answer to let the algorithm do its thing, you weren't allowed to skip questions or go back to change answers. On the revised GRE, the adapting will occur from section-to-section (e.g., if you do well on the first verbal section, you will get a harder second verbal section) rather than from question-to-question. The only change test takers will notice is one most will welcome: you can now move freely about the questions in a section, skipping tough questions and coming back to them later, changing answers after "ah-ha!" moments, and generally managing your time more flexibly.

The scores for the revised GRE Quantitative Reasoning and Verbal Reasoning will be reported on a 130 to 170 scale in 1-point increments, whereas the old score reporting was on a 200 to 800 scale in 10-point increments. You will receive one 130–170 score for verbal and a separate 130–170 score for quant. If you are already putting your GRE math skills to work, you may notice that there are now 41 scores possible (170 − 130, then add one before you're done), whereas before there were 61 scores possible ([800 − 200]/10, then add one before you're done). In other words, a 10 point difference on the old score scale actually indicated a smaller performance differential than a 1 point difference on the new scale. However, the GRE folks argue that perception is reality: the difference between 520 and 530 on the old scale could simply *seem* greater than the difference between 151 and 152 on the new scale. If that's true, then this change will benefit test-takers, who won't be unfairly compared by schools for minor differences in performance. If not true, then the change will be moot.

Important Dates

Registration for the GRE revised General Test opens on March 15, 2011, and the first day of testing with the new format is August 1, 2011.

Perhaps to encourage people to take the revised exam, rather than rushing to take the old exam before the change or waiting "to see what happens" with the new exam long after August 1, 2011, ETS is offering a 50% discount on the test fee for anyone who takes the revised test from August 1 through September 30, 2011. Scores for people who take

the revised exam in this discount period will be sent starting in mid- to late-November. This implies that you may have to wait up to 3.5 months to get your score during this rollout period!

By December 2011, ETS expects to resume normal score reporting schedules: score reports will be sent a mere 10-15 days after the test date.

IMPORTANT: If you need GRE scores before mid-November 2011 to meet a school deadline, take the "old" GRE no later than July 31, 2011! Waiting to take the revised test not only would require you to study for a different test, but also would delay your score reporting.

Question Formats in Detail

Essay Questions

The Analytical Writing section consists of two separately timed 30-minute tasks: Analyze an Issue and Analyze an Argument. As you can imagine, the 30-minute time limit implies that you aren't aiming to write an essay that would garner a Pulitzer Prize nomination, but rather to complete the tasks adequately and according to the directions. Each essay is scored separately, but your reported essay score is the average of the two rounded *up* to the next half-point increment on a 0 to 6 scale.

Issue Task—This essay prompt will present a claim, generally one that is vague enough to be interpreted in various ways and discussed from numerous perspectives. Your job as a test taker is to write a response discussing the extent to which you agree or disagree and support your position. Don't sit on the fence—pick a side!

For some examples of Issue Task prompts, visit the GRE website here:

http://www.ets.org/gre/revised_general/prepare/analytical_writing/issue/pool

Argument Task—This essay prompt will be an argument comprised of both a claim(s) and evidence. Your job is to dispassionately discuss the argument's structural flaws and merits (well, mostly the flaws). Don't agree or disagree with the argument—evaluate its logic.

For some examples of Argument Task prompts, visit the GRE website here:

http://www.ets.org/gre/revised_general/prepare/analytical_writing/argument/pool

Verbal: Reading Comprehension Questions

Standard 5-choice multiple choice reading comprehension questions will continue to appear on the new exam. You are likely familiar with how these work. Let's take a look at two *new* reading comprehension formats that will appear on the new test.

Select One or More Answer Choices and Select-in-Passage

For the question type, "Select One or More Answer Choices," you are given three statements about a passage and asked to "select all that apply." Either one, two, or all three can be correct (there is no "none of the above" option). There is no partial credit; you must select all the correct choices and none of the incorrect choices.

Strategy Tip: On "Select One or More Answer Choices," don't let your brain be tricked into telling you "Well, if two of them have been right so far, the other one must be wrong," or any other arbitrary idea about how many of the choices "should" be correct. Make sure to consider each choice independently! You cannot use "Process of Elimination" the same way as you do on "normal" multiple-choice questions.

For the question type "Select-in-Passage," you are given an assignment such as "Select the sentence in the passage that explains why the experiment's results were discovered to be invalid." Clicking anywhere on the sentence in the passage will highlight it. (As with any GRE question, you will have to click "Confirm" to submit your answer, so don't worry about accidentally selecting the wrong sentence due to a slip of the mouse.)

Strategy Tip: On "Select-in-Passage," if the passage is short, consider numbering each sentence (that is, writing 1 2 3 4 on your paper) and crossing off each choice as you determine that it isn't the answer. If the passage is long, you might write a number for each paragraph (I, II, III), and tick off each number as you determine that the correct sentence is not located in that paragraph.

Now let's give these new question types a try!

The sample questions below are based on this passage:

> Physicist Robert Oppenheimer, director of the fateful Manhattan Project, said "It is a profound and necessary truth that the deep things in science are not found because they are useful; they are found because it was possible to find them." In a later address at MIT, Oppenheimer presented the thesis that scientists could be held only very nominally responsible for the consequences of their research and discovery. Oppenheimer asserted that ethics, philosophy, and politics have very little to do with the day-to-day work of the scientist, and that scientists could not rationally be expected to predict all the effects of their work. Yet, in a talk in 1945 to the Association of Los Alamos Scientists, Oppenheimer offered some reasons why the Manhattan project scientists built the atomic bomb; the justifications included "fear that Nazi Germany would build it first" and "hope that it would shorten the war."

For question #1, consider each of the three choices separately and select all that apply.

1. The passage implies that Robert Oppenheimer would most likely have agreed with which of the following views:

    [A] Some scientists take military goals into account in their work
    [B] Deep things in science are not useful
    [C] The everyday work of a scientist is only minimally involved with ethics

2. Select the sentence in which the writer implies that Oppenheimer has not been consistent in his view that scientists have little consideration for the effects of their work.

[Here, you would highlight the appropriate sentence with your mouse. Note that there are only four options.]

Solutions:

1. {A, C}   Oppenheimer says in the last sentence that one of the reasons the bomb was built was scientists' "hope that it would shorten the war." Thus, Oppenheimer would likely agree with the view that "Some scientists take military goals into account in their work." B is a trap answer using familiar language from the passage. Oppenheimer says that scientific discoveries' possible usefulness is not why scientists make discoveries; he does not say that the discoveries aren't useful. Oppenheimer specifically says that ethics has "very little to do with the day-to-day work of the scientist," which is a good match for "only minimally involved with ethics."

    Strategy Tip: On "Select One or More Answer Choices," write ABC on your paper and mark each choice with a check, an X, or a symbol such as ~ if you're not sure. This should keep you from crossing out all three choices and having to go back (at least one of the choices must be correct). For example, let's say that on a different question you had marked

    A. X
    B. X
    C. ~

    The one you weren't sure about, (C), is likely to be correct, since there must be at least one correct answer.

2. The correct sentence is: **Yet, in a talk in 1945 to the Association of Los Alamos Scientists, Oppenheimer offered some reasons why the Manhattan project scientists built the atomic bomb; the justifications included "fear that Nazi Germany would build it first" and "hope that it would shorten the war."** The word "yet" is a good clue that this sentence is about to express a view contrary to the views expressed in the rest of the passage.

Verbal: Text Completion Questions

Text Completions are the new, souped-up Sentence Completions. They can consist of 1–5 sentences with 1–3 blanks. When Text Completions have two or three blanks, you will select words for those blanks independently. There is no partial credit; you must make every selection correctly.

Because this makes things a bit harder, the GRE has kindly reduced the number of possible choices per blank from five to three. Here is an old two-blank Sentence Completion, as it would appear on the old GRE:

Old Format:

> Leaders are not always expected to _____ the same rules as are those they lead; leaders are often looked up to for a surety and presumption that would be viewed as _____ in most others.
>
>   A.   obey … avarice
>
>   B.   proscribe … insalubriousness
>
>   C.   decree … anachronism
>
>   D.   conform to … hubris
>
>   E.   follow … eminence

And here's how this same sentence would appear on the new exam.

New Format:

> Leaders are not always expected to (i) _____ the same rules as are those they lead; leaders are often looked up to for a surety and presumption that would be viewed as (ii) _____ in most others.

Blank (i)
decree
proscribe
conform to

Blank (ii)
hubris
avarice
anachronism

On the new GRE, you will select your two choices by actually clicking and highlighting the words you want.

Solution:

In the first blank, we need a word similar to "follow." In the second blank, we need a word similar to "arrogant." Only choice D works in the old format; in the new format, the answer is still "conform to" and "hubris," but you'll make the two choices separately.

Note that in the "Old Format" question, if you knew that you needed a word in the second blank that meant something like "arrogant," and you knew that "hubris" was the only word in the second column with the correct meaning, you could pick correct answer choice D without even considering the first word in each pair. In the new format, this strategy is no longer available to us.

Also note that, in the "Old Format" question, "obey," "conform to," and "follow" mean basically the same thing. On the new GRE, this can't happen: since you select each word independently, no two choices can be synonyms (otherwise, there would be two correct answers).

Strategy Tip: As on the old GRE, do NOT look at the answer choices until you've decided for yourself, based on textual clues actually written in the sentence, what kind of word needs to go in each blank. Only then should you look at the choices and eliminate those that are not matches.

Let's try an example with three blanks.

> For Kant, the fact of having a right and having the (i) _____ to enforce it via coercion cannot be separated, and he asserts that this marriage of rights and coercion is compatible with the freedom of everyone. This is not at all peculiar from the standpoint of modern political thought—what good is a right if its violation triggers no enforcement (be it punishment or (ii) _____)? The necessity of coercion is not at all in conflict with the freedom of everyone, because this coercion only comes into play when someone has (iii)_____ someone else.

Blank (ii)	Blank (ii)	Blank (iii)
technique	amortization	questioned the hypothesis of
license	reward	violated the rights of
prohibition	restitution	granted civil liberties to

Solution:

In the first sentence, use the clue "he asserts that this marriage of rights and coercion is compatible with the freedom of everyone" to help fill in the first blank. Kant believes that "coercion" is "married to" rights and is compatible with freedom for all. So we want something in the first blank like "right" or "power." Kant believes that rights are meaningless without enforcement. Only the choice "license" can work (while a "license" can be physical, like a driver's license, "license" can also mean "right").

The second blank is part of the phrase "punishment or _____," which we are told is the "enforcement" resulting from the violation of a right. So the blank should be something, other than punishment, that constitutes enforcement against someone who violates a right. (More simply, it should be something bad!) Only "restitution" works. Restitution is compensating the victim in some way (perhaps monetarily or by returning stolen goods).

In the final sentence, "coercion only comes into play when someone has _____ someone else." Throughout the text, "coercion" means enforcement against someone who has violated the rights of someone else. The meaning is the same here. The answer is "violated the rights of."

The complete and correct answer is this combination:

Blank (i)	Blank (ii)	Blank (iii)
license	restitution	violated the rights of

In theory, there are $3 \times 3 \times 3 = 27$ possible ways to answer a 3-blank Text Completion—and only one of those 27 ways is correct. The guessing odds will go down, but don't be intimidated. Just follow the basic process: come up with your own filler for each blank, and match to the answer choices. If you're confused by this example, don't worry! We'll start from the beginning in our *Text Completion & Sentence Equivalence* strategy guide.

Strategy Tip: As on the old GRE, do NOT "write your own story." The GRE cannot give you a blank without also giving you a clue, physically written down in the passage, telling you what kind of word or phrase MUST go in that blank. Find that clue. You should be able to give textual evidence for each answer choice you select.

Verbal: Sentence Equivalence Questions

In this question type, you are given one sentence with a single blank. There are six answer choices, and you are asked to pick TWO choices that fit the blank and are alike in meaning.

Of the new question types, this one depends the most on vocabulary and also yields the most to strategy.

No partial credit is given on Sentence Equivalence; both correct answers must be selected. When you pick two of six choices, there are 15 possible combinations of choices, and only one is correct. However, this is not nearly as daunting as it sounds.

Think of it this way—if you have six choices, but the two correct ones must be "similar in meaning," then you have, at most, three possible PAIRS of choices. Maybe fewer, since not all choices are guaranteed to have a "partner." If you can match up the "pairs," you can seriously narrow down your options.

Here is a sample set of answer choices:

A   tractable

B   taciturn

C   arbitrary

D   tantamount

E   reticent

F   amenable

We haven't even given you the question here, because we want to point out how much you can do with the choices alone, if you have studied vocabulary sufficiently.

TRACTABLE and AMENABLE are synonyms (tractable, amenable people will do whatever you want them to do). TACITURN and RETICENT are synonyms (both mean "not talkative"). ARBITRARY (based on one's own will) and TANTAMOUT (equivalent) are not similar in meaning and therefore cannot be a pair. Therefore, the ONLY possible answers are {A, F} and {B, E}. We have improved our chances from 1 in 15 to a 50/50 shot without even reading the question!

Of course, in approaching a Sentence Equivalence, we do want to analyze the sentence the same way we would with a Text Completion—read for a textual clue that tells you what type of word MUST go in the blank. Then look for a matching pair.

Strategy Tip: If you're sure that a word in the choices does NOT have a partner, cross it out! For instance, if A and C are partners, and E and F are partners, and you're sure B and D are not each other's partners, cross out B and D completely. They cannot be the answer together, nor can either one be part of the answer.

The sentence for the answer choice above could read,

Though the dinner guests were quite _____ , the hostess did her best to keep the conversation active and engaging.

Thus, B and E are the best choices. Let's try an example.

While athletes usually expect to achieve their greatest feats in their teens or twenties, opera singers don't reach the _____ of their vocal powers until middle age.

A   harmony

B   zenith

C   acme

D   terminus

E   nadir

F   cessation

Solution:

Those with strong vocabularies might go straight to the choices to make pairs. ZENITH and ACME are synonyms, meaning "high point, peak." TERMINUS and CESSATION are synonyms, meaning "end." NADIR is a low point and HARMONY is present here as a trap answer reminding us of opera singers. *Cross off A and E, since they do not have partners.* Then, go back to the sentence, knowing that your only options are a pair meaning "peak" and a pair meaning "end."

The answer is {B, C}.

Math: Quantitative Comparison

This format is a holdover from the old exam. Here's a quick example:

<u>**Quantity A**</u>   <u>**Quantity B**</u>

x x^2

(A) Quantity A is greater.
(B) Quantity B is greater.
(C) The two quantities are equal.
(D) The relationship cannot be determined from the information given.

Solution: If $x = 0$, the quantities are equal. If $x = 2$, quantity B is greater. Thus, we don't have enough information.

The answer is D.

Let's look at the new math question formats.

Math: Select One or More Answer Choices

According to the *Official Guide to the GRE Revised General Test*, the official directions for "Select One or More Answer Choices" read as follows:

> <u>Directions:</u> Select one or more answer choices according to the specific question directions.
>
> If the question does not specify how many answer choices to select, select all that apply.
>
> The correct answer may be just one of the choices or as many as all of the choices, depending on the question.
>
> No credit is given unless you select all of the correct choices and no others.
>
> If the question specifies how many answer choices to select, select exactly that number of choices.

Note that there is no "partial credit." If three of six choices are correct and you select two of the three, no credit is given. It will also be important to read the directions carefully.

That said, many of these questions look *very* similar to those on the "old" GRE. For instance, here is a question that could have appeared on the GRE in the past:

If $ab = |a| \times |b|$, which of the following *must* be true?

    I. $a = b$
    II. $a > 0$ and $b > 0$
    III. $ab > 0$

    A.   II only
    B.   III only
    C.   I and III only
    D.   II and III only
    E.   I, II, and III

Solution: If $ab = |a| \times |b|$, then we know ab is positive, since the right side of the equation must be positive. If ab is positive, however, that doesn't necessarily mean that a and b are each positive; it simply means that they have the same sign.

    I.   It is not true that a must equal b. For instance, a could be 2 and b could be 3.
    II.   It is not true that a and b must each be positive. For instance, a could be −3 and b could be −4.
    III.   True. Since $|a| \times |b|$ must be positive, ab must be positive as well.

The answer is B (III only).

Note that, if you determined that statement I was false, you could eliminate choices C and E before considering the remaining statements. Then, if you were confident that II was also false, you could safely pick answer choice B, III only, without even trying statement III, since "None of the above" isn't an option. That is, because of the multiple choice answers, it is sometimes not necessary to consider each statement individually. This is the aspect of such problems that will change on the new exam.

Here is the same problem, in the new format.

If $ab = |a| \times |b|$, which of the following *must* be true?

Indicate <u>all</u> such statements.

    A $a = b$
    B $a > 0$ and $b > 0$
    C $ab > 0$

Strategy Tip: Make sure to fully "process" the statement in the question (simplify it or list the possible scenarios) before considering the answer choices. This will save you time in the long run!

Here, we would simply select choice C. The only thing that has changed is that we can't do process of elimination; we must always consider each statement individually. On the upside, the problem has become much more straightforward and compact (not every real-life problem has exactly five possible solutions; why should those on the GRE?).

Math: Numeric Entry

This question type requires the text taker to key a numeric answer into a box on the screen. You are not able to "work backwards" from answer choices, and in many cases it will be difficult to make a guess. However, the principles being tested are the same as on the old GRE.

Here is a sample question:

If $x*y = 2xy - (x - y)$, what is the value of 3*4?

Solution:

We are given a function involving two variables, x and y, and asked to substitute 3 for x and 4 for y:

$$x*y = 2xy - (x - y)$$
$$3*4 = 2(3)(4) - (3 - 4)$$
$$3*4 = 24 - (-1)$$
$$3*4 = 25$$

The answer is 25.

Thus, you would type 25 into the box.

Okay. You've now got a good start on understanding the structure and question formats of the new GRE. Now it's time to begin fine-tuning your skills.

PART 1: QUANTITATIVE COMPARISONS

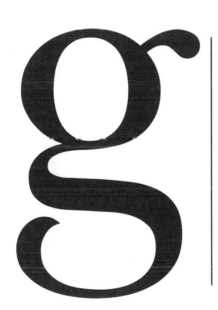

Chapter 2
of

QUANTITATIVE COMPARISONS &
DATA INTERPRETATION

THE BASICS

In This Chapter . . .

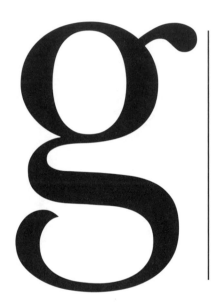

THE BASICS

Format and Directions

For quantitative comparison questions, you are to compare Quantity A with Quantity B and decide whether:

> **(A) Quantity A is greater.**
> **(B) Quantity B is greater.**
> **(C) The two quantities are equal.**
> **(D) The relationship cannot be determined from the information given.**

All of the first three answer choices have an implicit <u>ALWAYS</u> before the word "greater" or "equal". The answer choices can really be thought of this way:

> **(A) Quantity A is <u>ALWAYS</u> greater.**
> **(B) Quantity B is <u>ALWAYS</u> greater.**
> **(C) The two quantities are <u>ALWAYS</u> equal.**
> **(D) The relationship cannot be determined from the information given or no consistent relationship exists.**

Let's use an example problem to demonstrate this principle.

<u>Quantity A</u>	<u>Quantity B</u>
$x(10 - x)$	25

If x is any number other than 5, Quantity B will be bigger than Quantity A. For instance, if x is 4, then Quantity A is $4(6) = 24$. If x is 7, Quantity A is $7(3) = 21$.

At this stage, that means that answers choices A and C are no longer possible. We know that Quantity A is not <u>always</u> bigger, and we know the values in the two columns are not <u>always</u> equal.   A̸B∁̸D

But that doesn't mean the answer is B. When x is 5, Quantity A is $5(5) = 25$. In that case, the values in the two columns are equal. Although there are literally an infinite number of values of x that make Quantity B bigger, one counterexample is enough to make B the wrong answer. Quantity B is not <u>always</u> larger. This is a situation where the answer is D.

Trying to Prove D

This brings us to an important strategy that often comes into play when variables are involved. The secret is to always try to prove D, to look for those numbers that will work differently than the first numbers you consider.

In the search for numbers that will produce different results, there are some types of numbers that tend to be more useful than others. They are positive numbers, negative numbers, fractions between 0 and 1, fractions between 0 and −1, and the numbers −1, 0 and 1.

Negative Numbers	Negative Fractions	Positive Fractions	Positive Numbers
$x < 0$	$-1 < x < 0$	$0 < x < 1$	$x > 0$

$$-1 \qquad 0 \qquad 1$$

It may seem like a lot of work to test all of these ranges for every Quant Comp problem that involves variables, but there are a few things that can save you some time without preventing you from doing a thorough job.

The first thing that helps is that, as mentioned above, one counterexample is enough to make D the correct answer. As you get better at identifying which ranges of numbers will produce different results, you will shorten the amount of time spent answering the question.

The second thing that helps is that some problems provide constraints on the variables involved in the question. This helps by eliminating some possible ranges. Take this problem, for example.

y is an integer

Quantity A	**Quantity B**
$\dfrac{1}{2^y}$	$\dfrac{1}{3^y}$

y is an integer, so we know that we do not need to try positive and negative fractions. At the same time, we want to pick numbers that are easy to work with and will have a high potential impact. Let's begin with the number 1. If *y* equals 1, then Quantity A will be 1/2 and Quantity B will be 1/3. That means that Quantity A is bigger, and that B and C are no longer possible answer choices.   A̶B̶C̶D

Let's try another easy number: 0. If *y* = 0, then Quantity A is 1, because $2^0 = 1$. Similarly, Quantity B is 1, because 3^0 also equals 1. So the values of the two columns are equal. Therefore, A is no longer possible. We've found one case for which Quantity A is larger, and one for which the two quantities are equal. Thus, the correct answer is D.

0 was a good number to try for a couple of reasons. First, as mentioned, the calculations were easy to perform. Secondly, because the variable was an exponent, we were able to make use of the rule that any number when raised to a power of 0 equals 1. Even though we had two different bases, we managed to make them, and the columns, equal.

Compare, Don't Calculate

For a variety of reasons, ETS wants to ask questions on the Quantitative section of the GRE that quickly test your ability to reason about quantities, but that don't rely too much on raw computational ability. The Quantitative Comparison questions were developed specifically to fill this role. On many questions, you will be tempted to use the on-screen calculator, but using the calculator will often be more trouble than it's worth.

For the most part, the best way to approach Quantitative Comparison questions is to take advantage of the opportunities to avoid computation that the test-makers deliberately give you, and to avoid the traps that they deliberately set. Though some test-prep purveyors like to talk about "beating the test" or "cracking the code," the truth is that Educational Testing Service, the people who invented this format, and who write the GRE and SAT among many other tests, deliberately create opportunities for the savvy test-taker. This example problem will demonstrate the principle nicely.

Quantity A	**Quantity B**
$\dfrac{1}{\frac{1}{2}+\frac{1}{4}+\frac{1}{8}}$	$\dfrac{1}{2}+\dfrac{1}{4}+\dfrac{1}{8}$

On the surface, this problem seems to involve a lot of fractions that must be added together, which can be time consuming. On top of that, there is a complex fraction in Quantity A which could further slow us down. But there is no need for this level of computation. Notice that Quantity B, $\frac{1}{2}+\frac{1}{4}+\frac{1}{8}$, is less than $\frac{1}{2}+\left(\frac{1}{4}+\frac{1}{4}\right)$, and so must be less than 1. This means that the numerator in Quantity A (1) is greater than the denominator $\frac{1}{2}+\frac{1}{4}+\frac{1}{8}$, and so the entire fraction is greater than 1. We don't have to actually add the fractions in the expression $\frac{1}{2}+\frac{1}{4}+\frac{1}{8}$. The correct answer is A. (The fractions add up to $\frac{7}{8}$ by the way.)

In this problem, we determined the correct answer solely by making the distinction that Quantity B is less than 1, while Quantity A is greater than 1. Much of your preparation for Quantitative Comparisons will revolve around your ability to identify these quick distinctions that can save you time and energy spent performing unnecessary calculations. Try another example.

Quantity A	**Quantity B**
$\dfrac{1}{4}-\dfrac{1}{5}+\dfrac{1}{6}-\dfrac{1}{7}+\dfrac{1}{8}$	$\dfrac{1}{4}$

If you're tempted to actually evaluate the expression on the left with the calculator—STOP! It will take a lot of time and energy. In this case, all we need to do is compare the two values. The first fraction in the expression in Quantity A is $\frac{1}{4}$, which is the same as the fraction in Quantity B. All we have to do is determine whether the remaining fractions will increase or decrease our starting value, which is a lot less work.

We can group the remaining fractions into groups of two. What is the net effect of subtracting $\frac{1}{5}$ and adding $\frac{1}{6}$? $\frac{1}{5}$ is greater than $\frac{1}{6}$, so the net effect is negative. Similarly, subtracting $\frac{1}{7}$ and adding $\frac{1}{8}$ will also make the value smaller. Without knowing the exact value of the expression on the left, we can be sure that it will be smaller than the value on the right. The correct answer is B.

As you practice answering Quantitative Comparisons, you should always be on the lookout for ways to reduce the amount of computation required to arrive at an answer. To close out this section, we'll talk about some strategies that can be employed to reduce your workload on some QC questions.

The Invisible Inequality

Some QC problems are difficult simply because one or both of the columns are written in such a way that makes direct comparisons difficult. Take this problem, for example:

$$x > 0$$

Quantity A	**Quantity B**
$\dfrac{4x^2 + 2x^2 + 3x + 9}{2x}$	$2x + x + \dfrac{3}{2} + \dfrac{18}{4x}$

We could try plugging a number in for x, but it would be time consuming, even if we pick a simple number like 1. Additionally, how would plugging in a single number for x convince us that the conclusion was always valid? We would still need to try to prove D, taking yet more time.

Fortunately, there's a better way. All QC questions can be thought of as giant inequalities. To that end, there are a few things you're allowed to do to "both sides." You can:

    1) add or subtract the same value to both columns
    2) multiply or divide both columns by the same number, as long as it is positive
    3) square or square root both columns if you're sure they are both positive.

In this case, we're given a piece of common information telling us that $x > 0$. This is a signal telling you that you're allowed to multiply or divide both sides by x. On further thought, we'd probably be better off multiplying both columns by $2x$, because it will get rid of our denominator in Quantity A. Treat the two columns as if they are on opposite sides of an inequality. Because we don't know which direction the inequality faces, use a (?) as a place holder.

$$2x\left(\frac{4x^2+2x^2+3x+9}{2x}\right) \qquad ? \qquad 2x\left(2x+x+\frac{3}{2}+\frac{18}{4x}\right)$$

$$2\!\!\!/x\left(\frac{4x^2+2x^2+3x+9}{2\!\!\!/x}\right) \qquad ? \qquad 2x(2x)+2x(x)+2\!\!\!/x\left(\frac{3}{2\!\!\!/}\right)+2\!\!\!/x\left(\frac{18}{4\!\!\!/_2\,x\!\!\!/}\right)$$

$$4x^2+2x^2+3x+9 \qquad ? \qquad 4x^2+2x^2+3x+9$$

Our two columns are equal! We saved a whole lot of time by not plugging in numbers, so always keep the **invisible inequality** in mind. The answer is C.

Quantity B As Benchmark

Not to be confused with benchmark percents, using Quantity B as a benchmark can often provide us some insight into the problem at hand and save us some time. Take this problem, for example:

A discount of 30% off the original selling
price of a dress reduced the price to $99.

Quantity A	**Quantity B**
The original selling price	$150

There are two approaches to this problem. Both will get you there, but we want the method that will get you there most quickly. Instead of setting up an equation to solve for the original price of the sweater, assume the original price was $150, Quantity B.

 If the original price was $150, and it was reduced 30%, we can use the calculator to calculate the discounted price very quickly. 30% of 150 is $0.3 \cdot 150 = \$45$. That means the discounted price is $\$150 - \$45 = \$105$.

An original price of $150 with a 30% discount would have made the new price $105, which is higher than the discount price stipulated in the additional information. Therefore the original price of the sweater must have been less than $150. The answer is B.

If Quantity B is a number and Quantity A requires calculation of some kind, see if you can simplify equations and reduce the amount of necessary computation by using Quantity B as a benchmark.

Quantity B can also help in a slightly different, but related, way. Earlier in this chapter we talked about trying to prove D. Sometimes the best way to prove D is by trying to prove C using Quantity B as a guide.

✔ **Quantity A**	**Quantity B**
The perimeter of Triangle *ABC*, an isosceles triangle whose longest side is equal to 11.	22

Though there is no picture given, it should be easy to imagine a triangle that has a perimeter greater than 22. If one of the other sides also has a length of 11, then no matter the length of the third side, the perimeter will be greater than 22. So now our goal is to find a triangle that has a perimeter of 22 or less. 22 provides us with a goal, so that we do not have to search blindly and create random isosceles triangles that get us no closer to an answer.

If one of the sides is 11, that means that the remaining two sides must have a combined length of 11 if we are to achieve our goal. We have already seen what happens if the two equal sides each have a length of 11. Therefore, for the triangle to remain isosceles, the two unknown sides must be equal. The only way they could be equal is if they each have a length of 5.5.

Careful! There is a trap here. Remember, any two sides of a triangle must add up to GREATER than the length of the other side or else you can't actually connect all three sides. So this triangle cannot, in fact, exist. Similarly, the two sides cannot be less than 5.5, so we know that the perimeter of Triangle *ABC* will be greater than 22. The answer is A.

By specifically trying to make the two values equal, we were able to prove that Quantity A will always be greater. Trying to prove C saved us time by giving us a specific value to focus on.

If you are unsure of the geometry rules we used to solve this question, don't worry. You'll get a proper review in our *Geometry* strategy guide.

It is worth saying again that the strategies we've laid out are only some of the shortcuts available to a test taker with a trained eye. In general, your motto should be: Less is More. Good test-takers are always vigilant, always looking for ways to reduce their computational burden.

In the next section of this book, we'll explore areas of interest organized by content area: Algebra, FDPs, Geometry, Number Properties and Word Problems. Remember, this is still a math test, and a good understanding of fundamental rules and formulas is still essential to a good score.

Section Recap:

Some of the strategies you will be employing on Quantitative Comparisons are:

Try to Prove D
    Use −1, 0 and 1
    Use positive numbers greater than 1 and fractions between 0 and 1
    Use negative numbers less than −1 and fractions between 0 and −1

Use the Invisible Inequality
    Add or subtract to both columns
    Multiply or divide both columns by a positive number
    Square or square root both columns if they are positive

Use Quantity B as a Benchmark
    Use when Quantity B is a number (no variables)

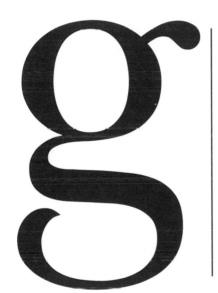

Chapter 3
of

QUANTITATIVE COMPARISONS &
DATA INTERPRETATION

ALGEBRA

In This Chapter . . .

- Equations
- Quadratic Equations
- Formulas
- Inequalities & Absolute Values

ALGEBRA

Finding quick solutions is a fairly general theme on QC, but nowhere is this theme more relevant than with algebra. If you generally associate algebra with long complicated equations, isolating variables, solving systems of equations with 2 or even 3 variables, etc., you're in for a treat. Bottom line: you will not have to do a lot of algebra on QC questions. This is not to say that Algebra questions are easier than questions in other content areas, but many equations that appear on QC can be simplified in just a few steps. Let's see how the GRE tests your understanding of algebraic principles on QC. Note that this chapter will assume basic familiarity with algebraic concepts and will only focus on principles of QC questions. For more specifics on algebraic concepts, see the Manhattan GRE Strategy Guide titled *Algebra*.

Equations

The most important thing you have to figure out on QC Algebra questions is when you are allowed to plug in a number, and when you are not. In other words, when is a variable not a variable?

Consider this example. Can we plug in numbers?

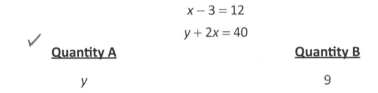

$$x - 3 = 12$$
$$y + 2x = 40$$

Quantity A	Quantity B
y	9

Pay attention to any constraints that have been placed on variables. In this question, the first equation gives us enough information to find the value of x. And because we have enough information to find x, we also have enough information to find y through the second equation. In fact, $x = 15$, which means that y will equal 10, and thus the answer to this question is A. Although y is a variable, it actually has a definite value.

Problem Recap: When variables have a UNIQUE VALUE, you must SOLVE for the value of the variable.

On this test, variables can assume a variety of forms. They can:

    1) have one unique value (as in the problem above)
    2) have a range of possible values (i.e. $-3 < z < 2$)
    3) have no constraints
    4) be defined in terms of other variables

On any question that involves variables, you should identify which situation you are dealing with. Take this problem, for instance.

$$2 \leq z \leq 4$$

Quantity A	Quantity B
$\dfrac{2z}{5}$	$\dfrac{5}{2z}$

In this problem, z doesn't have one specific value, but its range is well-defined. In a situation such as this, we should examine the upper and lower bounds of z.

Start with the lower bound. Plug in 2 for z in both columns.

$$2 \leq z \leq 4$$

Quantity A	**Quantity B**
$\dfrac{2(2)}{5} = \dfrac{4}{5}$	$\dfrac{5}{2(2)} = \dfrac{5}{4}$

When $z = 2$, Quantity B is bigger.   A̷B₵̷D

Now try the upper bound. Plug in 4 for z in both columns.

$$2 \leq z \leq 4$$

Quantity A	**Quantity B**
$\dfrac{2(4)}{5} = \dfrac{8}{5}$	$\dfrac{5}{2(4)} = \dfrac{5}{8}$

When $z = 4$, Quantity A is bigger. The correct answer is D.

The way in which variables are constrained (or not) can tell you a lot about efficient ways to approach that particular problem.

Problem Recap: If a variable has a DEFINED RANGE, you need to test the BOUNDARIES of that range.

Relationship Only

Another way variables can be defined on this test is in terms of another variable. Take the following example:

$$\frac{x+5}{5} = \frac{y+6}{6}$$

Quantity A	**Quantity B**
$6x$	$5y$

In this problem, we are given an equation that contains two variables: x and y. We won't be able to solve for the value of either variable, but that doesn't mean the answer will be D. For this type of problem, our best course of action is to make a DIRECT COMPARISON of the variables. We can do this by SIMPLIFYING the equation so that all unnecessary terms have been eliminated. We should begin by cross-multiplying:

$6(x + 5) = 5(y + 6)$
$6x + 30 = 5y + 30$

Now we have a 30 on each side that should be eliminated:

$6x = 5y$

We still don't know the value of either variable, but we do have enough information to answer the question. The answer is C.

Problem Recap: If a variable is defined in terms of another variable, SIMPLIFY and find a DIRECT COMPARISON.

No Constraints

Sometimes, you will not be given any information about a variable. If there are no constraints on the variable, then your goal is to PROVE D.

Quantity A	**Quantity B**
$\dfrac{x}{2}$	$2x$

No information about x has been given. If x is positive, Quantity B will be bigger. For instance, if $x = 1$, Quantity A =

$\dfrac{1}{2}$ and Quantity B = 4.   A̸B$\not\!C$D

However, there is no reason x must be positive. Remember, one way to try to prove D is to check negative possibilities.

If x is negative, then Quantity A will be bigger. For instance, if $x = -1$, then Quantity A = $-\dfrac{1}{2}$ and Quantity B = -2.

A̸$\not\!B$$\not\!C$D

The correct answer is D.

Problem Recap: If a variable has no constraints, TRY TO PROVE D.

Certain Properties

Finally, variables may be defined as having certain properties. The most common include a variable being positive or negative or an integer. The strategy for this type of problem is identical to the strategy for problems in which variables have no constraints: PROVE D. The only difference is that the types of numbers you can use are restricted. This type is also similar to Range of Values, in that you should test extreme values of the possible range.

x is positive

Quantity A	**Quantity B**
$x(x + 1)$	$x(x^2 + 1)$

Begin by distributing both columns:

x is positive

Quantity A	**Quantity B**
$x(x + 1) = x^2 + x$	$x(x^2 + 1) = x^3 + x$

Both sides have an x, which we can cancel out.

Quantity A		**Quantity B**

x is positive

$$
\begin{array}{r}
x^2 + x \\
-x \\
\hline
x^2
\end{array}
\qquad\qquad
\begin{array}{r}
x^3 + x \\
-x \\
\hline
x^3
\end{array}
$$

We know x is positive, so x can't be negative or 0. If $x = 2$, then Quantity A = 4 and Quantity B = 8.   ̶A̶B̶ ̶C̶ D

In order to be thorough, however, we need to make sure that we try numbers that have a chance of behaving differently. We can't try negatives, but we can try 1 and fractions between 0 and 1. If $x = 1$, then Quantity A = 1 and Quantity B = 1. Also, if x were a positive fraction (e.g. 1/2) then Quantity A would be greater than Quantity B. The correct answer is D.

Section Recap:

Variables are used in many ways on this test. How they're presented can often give you a clue as to the appropriate strategy to employ. To recap:

If a variable:	then:
has a UNIQUE VALUE (e.g. $x + 3 = -5$)	SOLVE for the value of the variable
has a DEFINED RANGE (e.g. $-4 \le w \le 3$)	test the BOUNDARIES
has a RELATIONSHIP with another variable (e.g. $2p = r$)	SIMPLIFY the equation and make a DIRECT COMPARISON of the variables
has NO CONSTRAINTS	try to PROVE D
has CERTAIN PROPERTIES (e.g. x is negative)	try to PROVE D

Quadratic Equations

We can boil the issue of quadratic equations down to one principle: know how to FOIL well. Many questions concerning quadratic equations hinge on your ability to FOIL factored expressions correctly.

The quadratic equation can appear either in one or both of the columns OR in the common information. Where it is will determine how you approach the question.

Quadratics in Columns

If the quadratic equation appears in the columns, then your goal is to FOIL and eliminate common terms to make a direct comparison.

$$pq \neq 0$$

Quantity A	**Quantity B**
$(2p + q)(p + 2q)$	$p^2 + 5pq + q^2$

In order to make a meaningful comparison between the two columns, we have no choice but to FOIL Quantity A.

We get:

> **F**irst $= 2p \cdot p = 2p^2$
> **O**utside $= 2p \cdot 2q = 4pq$
> **I**nside $= q \cdot p = pq$
> **L**ast $= q \cdot 2q = 2q^2$

The expression on the left equals $2p^2 + 5pq + 2q^2$. Both columns contain the term $5pq$, which we can safely subtract. The comparison becomes:

$$pq \neq 0$$

Quantity A	**Quantity B**
$2p^2 + 5pq + 2q^2$	$p^2 + 5pq + q^2$
$\underline{\quad -5pq \quad}$	$\underline{\quad -5pq \quad}$
$\mathbf{2p^2 \quad + 2q^2}$	$p^2 \quad + q^2$

The information at the top tells us that neither p nor q can be 0, and we know that p^2 and q^2 will both be positive, so we can now definitively say that Quantity A is larger than Quantity B. To answer this question correctly, we had to do two things: 1) FOIL Quantity A (the faster the better) and 2) eliminate common terms from both columns and compare the remaining terms. The correct answer is A.

As QC questions involving quadratic equations get more difficult, they can make either FOILing or simplifying more difficult. Try this example problem.

$$r > s$$

Quantity A	**Quantity B**
$(r + s)(r - s)$	$(s + r)(s - r)$

This problem now requires us to FOIL two expressions, not just one (we can't simply divide out $(r + s)$ from each side, because $(r + s)$ might be negative). However, this is where our knowledge of special products can save us some time. Each of these expressions is a difference of squares.

$$r > s$$

Quantity A	**Quantity B**
$(r + s)(r - s) = r^2 - s^2$	$(s + r)(s - r) = s^2 - r^2$

Now we need to be able to compare these expressions. We know r is greater than s, so it might be tempting to conclude that Quantity A is greater than Quantity B. Plug in $r = 3$ and $s = 2$.

$$r > s$$

Quantity A	**Quantity B**
$r^2 - s^2 =$	$s^2 - r^2 =$
$9 - 4 = 5$	$4 - 9 = -5$

Quantity A is greater than Quantity B.   A~~B~~~~C~~D

But there's a problem. We know r is greater than s, but we don't know the sign of either variable. Remember to check negative possibilities!

Now plug in $r = -2$ and $s = -3$.

$$r > s$$

Quantity A	**Quantity B**
$r^2 - s^2 =$	$s^2 - r^2 =$
$4 - 9 = -5$	$9 - 4 = 5$

We come to the opposite conclusion, that Quantity B is greater than Quantity A. Because we can't arrive at a consistent conclusion, the answer is D.

Problem Recap: The challenging part of this question was comparing the columns after we had FOILed them. Notice we had to incorporate our knowledge of positives and negatives to come to the correct conclusion. Harder questions will be difficult for either of two reasons:

> 1) expressions are hard to FOIL or
> 2) the comparisons are challenging

Quadratics in Common Information

Questions that contain quadratic equations in the common information will present different challenges.

$$x^2 - 6x + 8 = 0$$

Quantity A	**Quantity B**
x^2	2^x

The first thing to note here is that there will be two possible values for x. But we should not jump to conclusions and assume the answer will be D. To make sure we get the right answer, we need to solve for both values of x and plug them BOTH into the columns.

First, solve for x. We can factor the expression so that it reads $(x - 2)(x - 4) = 0$.

That means that $x = 2$ or $x = 4$. Let's start by plugging 2 in for x in both columns:

Quantity A	**Quantity B**
$(2)^2 = 4$	$2^{(2)} = 4$

When $x = 2$, the columns are equal.   ~~A~~~~B~~CD

Now try $x = 4$:

Quantity A	Quantity B
$(4)^2 = \mathbf{16}$	$2^{(4)} = \mathbf{16}$

Even though there are two possible values for x, both of these values lead us to the same conclusion: the columns are equal. The correct answer is C.

Problem Recap: When the common information contains a quadratic equation, solve for BOTH possible values and put them into the columns.

Section Recap:

There are two types of questions involving quadratics. Each type will require a different approach. If a quadratic:

        I) appears in one or both columns
                a) FOIL the quadratic
                b) eliminate common terms
                b) compare the columns

        II) appears in the common information
                a) factor the equation and find BOTH solutions
                b) plug both solutions into the columns

Formulas

Although relatively rare, strange symbol formulas do appear in Quantitative Comparison questions. The fastest way to answer them will depend on whether the question uses numbers or variables.

If we are given the numbers to plug into a strange symbol formula, we will need to evaluate the formula to answer the question. Refer to the Algebra Strategy Guide for help on answering strange symbol formula questions.

If we are not given the numbers to plug in, our task is slightly different.

$$v\& = 2v - 1$$

Quantity A	Quantity B
$(v\&)\&$	$4v$

We could try plugging in different numbers, but we would have no way of knowing if the answer we got was always true. And trying multiple numbers would be tedious and time consuming. Instead, evaluate the formula using the variable itself. Start by evaluating the formula inside the parentheses

$$v\& = 2v - 1$$

Rewrite Quantity A as $(2v - 1)\&$. Evaluate the formula one more time.

$$(2v - 1)\& = 2(2v - 1) - 1$$

$$= 4v - 2 - 1$$
$$= 4v - 3$$

Now our comparison looks like this:

Quantity A	**Quantity B**
$4v - 3$	$4v$
$-4v$	$-4v$
-3	0

Now, no matter what v is, we know that Quantity B will be bigger.

By spending the time to evaluate the formula using the variable v, we were able to save time at the end of the problem. Once the formula was evaluated, a clear comparison could be made between the columns.

Section Recap:

If a Quantitative Comparison question with a strange symbol formula contains NUMBERS, PLUG IN the numbers and evaluate the formula. If the question DOES NOT contain numbers, plug the given VARIABLE directly into the formula to compare the columns.

Inequalities & Absolute Values

Inequalities are a common theme in Quantitative Comparisons, and can take many forms. As we saw earlier in this section, one thing inequalities can do is restrict the range of a variable. Another way they are used is in combination with absolute values.

$$-2 \leq x \leq 3$$
$$-3 \leq y \leq 2$$

Quantity A	**Quantity B**
The maximum value of $|x - 4|$	The maximum value of $|y + 4|$

Once again, inequalities are used to bound a variable. As before, we should test the BOUNDARIES of the range. But now we have the added twist of absolute values. On QC, it is important to understand how to maximize and minimize values. The smallest possible value of any absolute value will be 0. *It is impossible for an absolute value to have a value less than 0.*

This question asks us to maximize the absolute values in Quantities A and B. In Quantity B, the maximum value of $|y + 4|$ will be when $y = 2$, because that is the largest number we can add to positive 4. The absolute value of $|y + 4|$ will equal 6.

To maximize the absolute value of $|x - 4|$ in Quantity A, however, we have to do the opposite. There is a negative 4 already in the absolute value. If we try to increase the value by adding a positive number to -4, we will only make the absolute value smaller. For instance, if x is 3, then the absolute value is

$$|3 - 4| = |-1| = 1$$

We can actually maximize the absolute value by making $x = -2$. Then the absolute value becomes

$$|-2 - 4| = |-6| = 6$$

Since the maximum value in each column is the same (6), the answer is C.

Remember, *if you need to maximize an absolute value, you need to make the number inside as far away from 0 as possible.* If the number is positive, then adding to it will increase the absolute value. To increase the value of $|y + 4|$, we made y positive. However, to increase the absolute value of $|x - 4|$, we needed to make x negative.

Problem Recap: When absolute values contain variables, manipulate the expression inside to make the absolute value larger or smaller.

Relative Order

The GRE often uses inequalities to show much more than the range of possible values for a variable. For instance, the common information may tell you that $0 < p < q < r$.

This inequality has told us two crucial things: 1) p, q and r are all positive and 2) p, q and r are in order from least to greatest.

Questions that provide this type of information will often use different combinations of these variables in each quantity and perform some kind of mathematical operation on them (e.g. $+$, $-$, $\times$, $\div$). We now have to LOOK FOR THE PATTERN.

If there is a pattern, the answer will be A, B or C. If there is no pattern, the answer will be D. Make use of the Invisible Inequality to discern the pattern, if one is present. Let's look at four basic examples, one for each of the four basic mathematical operations ($+$, $-$, $\times$, $\div$).

Example 1:

$$0 < p < q < r$$

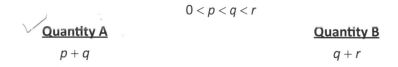

Quantity A	**Quantity B**
$p + q$	$q + r$

Pretend there is an unknown inequality between the two columns, designated by a (?).

$$0 < p < q < r$$

| $p + q$ | (?) | $q + r$ |

Both sides contain a q, so subtract the q:

$$0 < p < q < r$$

Quantity A		**Quantity B**
$p + q$	(?)	$q + r$
$\underline{-q}$		$\underline{-q}$
p		r

From the common information $(0 < p < q < r)$, we know that r is bigger than p, so Quantity B is definitely bigger.

Example 2:

$$0 < p < q < r$$

✓ **Quantity A**		**Quantity B**
pq	(?)	qr

Once again, both sides have a q. Because we know that q is positive, we can divide both sides by q without changing the Invisible Inequality.

$$0 < p < q < r$$

Quantity A		**Quantity B**
$\dfrac{pq}{q} = p$	(?)	$\dfrac{qr}{q} = r$

Once again, from the common information, we know that r is definitely greater than p. The correct answer is again B.

In both of the last two examples, we were able to successfully eliminate common terms to arrive at a definite conclusion.

However, take a look at the next example.

Example 3:

$$0 < p < q < r$$

✗ **Quantity A**		**Quantity B**
$q - p$	(?)	$r - q$

Both sides contain a q, but notice that their signs are different. We can't actually eliminate q altogether. If we try adding q to both sides, here's what we get:

$$0 < p < q < r$$

Quantity A		**Quantity B**
$q - p$		$r - q$
$\underline{+q}$	(?)	$\underline{+q}$
$2q - p$		r

Quantity A still contains q. Likewise, if we try subtracting q from both sides, we just push q into Quantity B.

$$0 < p < q < r$$

Quantity A		**Quantity B**
$q - p$		$r - q$
$\underline{-q}$	(?)	$\underline{-q}$
$-p$		$r - 2q$

Either way, we cannot arrive at a definite conclusion.

We can also pick numbers to show that there is no pattern. Remember to pick numbers satisfying $0 < p < q < r$. If $p = 1$, $q = 3$, and $r = 6$, then:

$$0 < p < q < r$$

Quantity A		**Quantity B**
$q - p = 3 - 1 = 2$	(?)	$r - q = 6 - 3 = 3$

With these numbers, Quantity B is bigger.   ~~ABCD~~

Now space the numbers differently. In the previous case, q was closer to p than to r. Try putting q closer to r than to p.

If $p = 2$, $q = 7$ and $r = 8$, then:

$$0 < p < q < r$$

Quantity A		**Quantity B**
$q - p = 7 - 2 = 5$	(?)	$r - q = 8 - 7 = 1$

Now Quantity A is bigger. The correct answer is D.

We find ourselves in a similar dilemma with this fourth example.

Example 4:

$$0 < p < q < r$$

✓ **Quantity A**		**Quantity B**
$\dfrac{q}{p}$	(?)	$\dfrac{r}{q}$

Because all the variables are positive, we can cross-multiply.

$$0 < p < q < r$$

Quantity A		**Quantity B**
q^2	(?)	pr

It's impossible to know for sure which column will be bigger. For extra practice, use numbers satisfying $0 < p < q < r$ to prove the answer is D. (Hint: space the numbers differently, as in the example above.)

Section Recap:

Sometimes inequalities are used to order variables from least to greatest. In the previous examples, the common information $(0 < p < q < r)$

      1) gave the sign of the variables and
      2) gave their order from least to greatest

To compare the two columns, use the Invisible Inequality to

      1) eliminate common terms and
      2) try to discern a pattern if one is present

Problem Set

1. $0 < x < 1$

Quantity A	**Quantity B**
$(x^3 - x)(4x + 3)$	$(x^2 + 1)(4x^2 + 3x)$

2. $6 \le m \le 12$

Quantity A	**Quantity B**
$9 - m$	$m - 9$

3.
$$\frac{\dfrac{-21}{2}m}{2} = \frac{7}{2}n$$

$$mn \ne 0$$

Quantity A	**Quantity B**
$3m$	$-n$

4.

Quantity A	**Quantity B**
x	$3x - 4$

5. $x^2 + x - 42 - 0$

Quantity A	**Quantity B**
$|x + 1|$	5

6.
$$@(x) = x^2 - 4$$

Quantity A	**Quantity B**
$@(10)$	$@(@(4))$

7.
$$\clubsuit x = \frac{1}{x-1}$$

Quantity A	**Quantity B**
$\clubsuit(\clubsuit x)$	$\dfrac{x-1}{2-x}$

8.
$$|x - 2| > 3$$

Quantity A	**Quantity B**
The minimum possible value of $|x - 3.5|$	The minimum possible value of $|x - 1.5|$

9.
$$a < b < 0 < c < d$$

Quantity A	**Quantity B**
abc	$c - d$

10.
$$0 < a < 1 < b < c$$

Quantity A	**Quantity B**
$\dfrac{c^2}{a}$	$\dfrac{bc}{ab}$

Answer Key

1. B   2. D   3. D   4. D   5. A   6. B   7. C   8. B   9. A   10. A

Solutions

1. **B:** Notice that in each of the columns, we can factor an x out of one of the expressions.

$$0 < x < 1$$

Quantity A	**Quantity B**
$(x^3 - x)(4x + 3) =$ $x(x^2 - 1)(4x + 3)$	$(x^2 + 1)(4x^2 + 3x) =$ $(x^2 + 1)(4x + 3)x$

Because we know that x is not 0, we can use the Invisible Inequality to divide away the common terms from both columns (x and $(4x + 3)$).

$$0 < x < 1$$

Quantity A	**Quantity B**
$x(x^2 - 1)(4x + 3) =$ $x^2 - 1$	$(x^2 + 1)(4x + 3)x =$ $x^2 + 1$

Now the comparison is easy to make. Because x^2 will always be positive, $(x^2 + 1)$ will always be bigger than $(x^2 - 1)$.

2. **D:** Try to prove D by Testing the Boundaries of the Range for m.

If $m = 6$, then Quantity A is equal to $9 - (6) = 3$, and Quantity B is equal to $(6) - 9 = -3$. Eliminate answer choices B and C.

If $m = 12$, then Quantity A is equal to $9 - (12) = -3$, and Quantity B is equal to $(12) - 9 = 3$. Eliminate answer choice A.

The answer is D.

3. **D:** Never leave a complex fraction in place—that is, simplify in order to find a direct comparison. First, multiply both sides by 2:

$$\dfrac{\dfrac{-21}{2}m}{2} = \dfrac{\dfrac{7}{2}n}{2} \quad \rightarrow \quad \dfrac{-21}{2}m = 7n$$

Multiply both sides by 2 again:

$$\dfrac{-21}{2}m = 7n \quad \rightarrow \quad -21m = 14n$$

Divide by -7 in order to make the left side of the equation $3m$ (Quantity A).

$-21m = 14n$ $\rightarrow$ $3m = -2n$

Since $3m = -2n$, we can substitute $-2n$ for $3m$ in Quantity A. The problem now reads:

$$mn \neq 0$$

Quantity A	**Quantity B**
$-2n$	$-n$

If n is positive, B is bigger. If n is negative, A is bigger.

The answer is D.

4. **D:** If there are no constraints on a variable, try to prove D.

If $x = 0$, Quantity A is equal to 0 and Quantity B is equal to -4. Eliminate answer choices B and C.
If $x = 10$, Quantity A is equal to 10 and Quantity B is equal to 26. Eliminate answer choice A.

The answer is D.

5. **A:** This question contains a quadratic equation in the common information. The first thing to note here is that there will be two possible values for x. But we should not jump to conclusions and assume the answer will be D. To make sure we get the right answer, we need to solve for both values of x and plug them BOTH into the columns.

$x^2 + x - 42 = 0$
$(x + 7)(x - 6) = 0$
$x = -7$ or 6

Now, the problem reads:

$$x = -7 \text{ or } 6$$

Quantity A	**Quantity B**
$|x + 1|$	5

If $x = -7$, Quantity A is equal to the absolute value of -6, which is 6, and Quantity B will still be equal to 5.
If $x = 6$, Quantity A is equal to the absolute value of 7, which is 7, and Quantity B will still be equal to 5.
In either case, Quantity A is bigger.

6. **B:** If a Quantitative Comparison question with a strange symbol formula contains numbers, PLUG IN the numbers and evaluate the formula.

In Quantity A, $@(10) = (10)^2 - 4 = 96$.

In Quantity B, work outwards from the "inner core." $@(4) = 4^2 - 4 = 12$. Now evaluate $@(12)$.

$@(12) = 12^2 - 4 = 140$.

Quantity B is bigger.

The answer is B.

7. **C:** Remember, if you are given a strange symbol on the GRE, the exam will have to define that strange symbol for you. Since we are not given numbers to plug in, we should evaluate the formula using the variable itself—otherwise, if we plugged in numbers, we would have no way of knowing whether we would have to try more numbers to try to prove D.

Quantity A asks us for $\clubsuit(\clubsuit x)$. They want us to plug the function into itself. So, plug $\dfrac{1}{x-1}$ in for x:

$$\cfrac{1}{\cfrac{1}{x-1}-1}$$

Combine the two terms in the denominator.

$$\cfrac{1}{\cfrac{1}{x-1}-1} \rightarrow \cfrac{1}{\dfrac{1}{x-1}-\dfrac{x-1}{x-1}} = \cfrac{1}{\dfrac{2-x}{x-1}}$$

Remember, if a fraction is under a 1, just flip it over:

$$\cfrac{1}{\dfrac{2-x}{x-1}} = \dfrac{x-1}{2-x}$$

The answer is C.

8. **B:** As with all absolute value equations or inequalities, here we must solve twice:

$|x-2| > 3$
$x-2 > 3$ OR $x-2 < -3$
$x > 5$ OR $x < -1$

Even better, we could express the possible values of x on a number line:

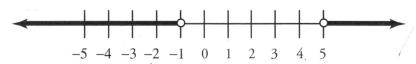

Quantity A is equal to the minimum possible value of $|x - 3.5|$. Another way to think of $|x - 3.5|$ is "the distance on a number line from x to 3.5." Look at 3.5 on the number line above, and note the nearest possible distance, which is "greater than 5" (x may not be exactly 5, but it could be 5.000001, for instance, since there is no requirement that it be an integer). Therefore, since the distance from 3.5 to "greater than 5" is "greater than 1.5," Quantity A is equal to "greater than 1.5." That is, the minimum possible value of $|x - 3.5|$ is 1.5 plus any very small amount—for instance, 1.5000001 would be a legal value.

Quantity B can be conceived as "the smallest distance from x to 1.5." Look at 1.5 on the number line—the nearest value is "less than −1," which is more than 2.5 units away. Thus, the minimum possible value of $|x - 1.5|$ is "greater than 2.5."

If Quantity A's minimum is just greater than 1.5 and Quantity B's minimum is just greater than 2.5, Quantity B is larger.

The answer is B.

You could also solve this problem by plugging in values, rather than using a number line. First, solve the inequality as above to get $x > 5$ or $x < -1$. Now try plugging "greater than 5," "less than −1," as well as very small and very large numbers—that is, the extremes of both ranges for x (although you may be able to use a bit of logic beforehand to tell that you only want values very close to 1.5 and 3.5) to make sure that you generate the smallest possible value for each column. Quantity A's smallest value will be smaller than Quantity B's smallest value.

The answer is B.

9. **A:** When variables are ordered from least to greatest, Look For The Pattern. Notice that a and b are negative, and c and d are positive. Try working only with positives and negatives first, before considering more specific numbers.

In Quantity A, abc is a negative times a negative times a positive—that is, Quantity A is a positive value.

In Quantity B, $c - d$ is a positive minus a positive. Now, a positive minus a positive can yield either a positive or a negative value (for instance 10 minus 1 versus 1 minus 10). So let's look back up at the common information to see that d is greater than c. Thus, $c - d$ is an instance of subtracting a larger positive from a smaller positive, which yields a negative.

Quantity A is positive and Quantity B is negative.

The answer is A.

10. **A:** When variables are ordered from least to greatest, look for the pattern. We can also use the technique of the Invisible Inequality—and since all of the variables are positive, we can cross-multiply across that invisible inequality.

$\dfrac{c^2}{a}$	?	$\dfrac{bc}{ab}$
abc^2	?	abc

Since we know a, b, and c are positive, go ahead and divide out abc:

c	?	1

We were directly told in the Common Information that $1 < c$, so Quantity A is bigger.

The answer is A.

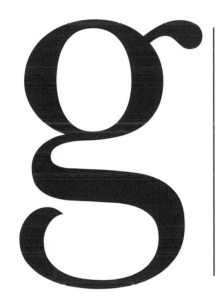

Chapter 4
of
QUANTITATIVE COMPARISONS &
DATA INTERPRETATION

FRACTIONS,
DECIMALS, &
PERCENTS

In This Chapter . . .

- Quick Elimination: Less Than 1 vs. Greater Than 1

- Simplifying Complex Fractions

- Fractions with Exponents—Plug in 0 and 1

- Percents

FRACTIONS, DECIMALS, & PERCENTS

Fractions are ubiquitous on the GRE, and you will need a variety of skills to deal with them properly. This chapter outlines some of the more common strategies you can employ to save time and get questions right. Again, you should expect to practice these strategies multiple times before you can consistently and naturally apply them.

Quick Elimination: Less Than 1 vs. Greater Than 1

Sometimes answering a question is as simple as asking, "Is this fraction greater or less than 1?" To answer this question, we just have to compare the numerator and the denominator.

$$n > 0$$

Quantity A	**Quantity B**
$\dfrac{n}{n+1}$	$\dfrac{n+1}{n}$

If n is positive, then so is $n + 1$. Both fractions have positive numerators and denominators. Now we can ask, "Is $\dfrac{n}{n+1}$ greater or less than 1?" Since $n + 1$ is bigger than n, we can quickly see that $\dfrac{n}{n+1}$ is less than 1. Likewise, we can quickly see that $\dfrac{n+1}{n}$ is greater than 1. The correct answer is B.

Problem Recap: It only takes a few seconds to ask whether each fraction is greater or less than 1. If this approach works, you have saved yourself time. If it does not work, you have only spent a few seconds and can quickly move to a new approach.

Simplifying Complex Fractions

Occasionally, a Quantitative Comparison has a complex fraction in one or both of the columns. A complex fraction is any fraction that has a fraction in either the numerator or denominator.

$$x > 0$$

Quantity A	**Quantity B**
$\dfrac{2+\dfrac{2}{3x}}{2}$	$\dfrac{3+\dfrac{3}{2x}}{3}$

A good first step is to SPLIT THE NUMERATOR.

$$x > 0$$

Quantity A	**Quantity B**

$$\dfrac{2 + \dfrac{2}{3x}}{2} =$$

$$\dfrac{2}{2} + \dfrac{\dfrac{2}{3x}}{2}$$

$$\dfrac{3 + \dfrac{3}{2x}}{3} =$$

$$\dfrac{3}{3} + \dfrac{\dfrac{3}{2x}}{3}$$

Splitting the Numerators is helpful because the denominator is just one term. Now it is easy to see that both columns contain a 1 (2/2 and 3/3 both equal 1). We can subtract 1 from both columns, because of the Invisible Inequality.

$$x > 0$$

Quantity A	**Quantity B**

$$\dfrac{2}{2} + \dfrac{\dfrac{2}{3x}}{2} =$$

$$\dfrac{\dfrac{2}{3x}}{2}$$

?

$$\dfrac{3}{3} + \dfrac{\dfrac{3}{2x}}{3} =$$

$$\dfrac{\dfrac{3}{2x}}{3}$$

Now we need to focus on the complex fractions in each column. The next step is to divide both fractions. Remember—fraction bars represent division. Also keep straight which is the "big" fraction bar.

$$\dfrac{\dfrac{3}{2x}}{3} \neq \dfrac{3}{\dfrac{2x}{3}}$$

One way to divide is to multiply by the reciprocal. The numerator of the fraction in Quantity A is being divided by 2.

That is the same as multiplying by the reciprocal of 2, which is $\dfrac{1}{2}$. We can do something similar with the fraction in Quantity B.

Quantity A	$x > 0$	**Quantity B**

$$\dfrac{\dfrac{2}{3x}}{2} =$$

$$\dfrac{2}{3x} \cdot \dfrac{1}{2}$$

$$\dfrac{\dfrac{3}{2x}}{3} =$$

$$\dfrac{3}{2x} \cdot \dfrac{1}{3}$$

Now we can simplify the expressions.

Quantity A	$x > 0$	**Quantity B**

$$\dfrac{\cancel{2}}{3x} \cdot \dfrac{1}{\cancel{2}} =$$

$$\dfrac{1}{3x}$$

$$\dfrac{\cancel{3}}{2x} \cdot \dfrac{1}{\cancel{3}} =$$

$$\dfrac{1}{2x}$$

Remember, as a positive denominator gets larger, the fraction gets smaller. Since $x > 0$, the denominator of $\dfrac{1}{3x}$ will always be bigger than the denominator of $\dfrac{1}{2x}$. Therefore the fraction in Quantity B will always be larger. B is the correct answer.

Problem Recap: When simplifying complex fractions, look to

    1) SPLIT THE NUMERATOR when the denominator is one term

    2) turn division into multiplication by the reciprocal (e.g. $\dfrac{2}{2/3} = 2 \cdot \dfrac{3}{2}$)

Fractions with Exponents—Plug in 0 and 1

Fractions containing exponents are challenging, but they can also present opportunities to save some time.

Quantity A	**Quantity B**
$\dfrac{1}{2^t}$	2^t

The first step is to plug in numbers. To save yourself time, always try the numbers 0 and 1 first (unless the common information rules out those values, such as by specifying that a variable is negative). Anything raised to the 0th power equals 1 (e.g. $2^0 = 1$). Anything raised to the 1st power equals itself.

If we plug 0 in for t, then the columns are:

Quantity A	**Quantity B**
$\dfrac{1}{2^0} = \dfrac{1}{1} = \mathbf{1}$	$2^0 = \mathbf{1}$

When $t = 0$, the columns are equal.   A̶B̶CD

Now plug in 1.

Quantity A	**Quantity B**
$\dfrac{1}{2^1} = \dfrac{\mathbf{1}}{\mathbf{2}}$	$2^1 = \mathbf{2}$

Now Quantity B is bigger. The correct answer is D.

Problem Recap: When fractions contain exponents and you have to plug in numbers for the exponents, always plug in 0 and 1 first to save yourself time.

Percents

The Original Value

An important consideration when dealing with percents is the size of the total that you are taking a percent of.

An item is discounted
by 20%, and then a 20%
surcharge is applied to
the discounted price

Quantity A	**Quantity B**
The price after the discount and surcharge	The original price

Two percent operations are performed. First, a price is discounted by 20%. The new price is now 80% of the original. Next, 20% is added to this new price. Two things are important to note here:

    1) The percent increase (as a *percentage*) is the same as the percent decrease and
    2) The percent increase is based on the NEW, smaller price

In dollar terms, the 20% increase will have to be smaller than the original 20% decrease, because we are adding 20% to a smaller number. Without any actual calculations, we can be confident that the price after the discount and the surcharge will be less than the original price.

We can also demonstrate this principle by picking a price for the item. As always, a good number to use when we work with percents is 100.

*ManhattanGRE*Prep
the new standard

The 20% discount is 20% of **100** = 0.2 × 100 = $20.

The new price is $100 − $20 = $80.

The 20% surcharge is 20% of **80** = 0.2 × 80 = $16. Use the calculator for this if you need to.

The final price is $80 + $16 = $96.

The original price ($100) is larger than the final price after the discount and surcharge ($96). The answer is B.

Problem Recap: When dealing with percents, always pay attention to the size of the original value. 20% of a small number is less than 20% of a larger number.

Problem Set

1. A town's population rose 40% from 2006 to 2007.
   The 2007 population was 10,080.

Quantity A	**Quantity B**
The 2006 population	7,000

2.

Quantity A	**Quantity B**
$\dfrac{1}{3}+\dfrac{1}{4}+\dfrac{7}{12}$	$\dfrac{1}{\dfrac{1}{3}+\dfrac{1}{4}+\dfrac{7}{12}}$

3.

Quantity A	**Quantity B**
$\dfrac{1}{6}-\left(\dfrac{1}{2}\right)^2+\left(-\dfrac{1}{4}\right)^2$	$\dfrac{1}{6}$

4.

Quantity A	**Quantity B**
$\dfrac{\dfrac{4}{3}+(-2)}{-2}$	$\dfrac{-\dfrac{4}{3}+2}{2}$

5. $x > 1$

Quantity A	**Quantity B**
$\dfrac{x+5}{x}$	$\dfrac{(x-1)+5}{x-1}$

√6.

$$x = -y$$
$$xy \neq 0$$

Quantity A	**Quantity B**
$\dfrac{5.5x^2}{5}$	$\dfrac{3y^2}{2.5}$

√7.

Quantity A	**Quantity B**
$(0.\overline{7})(0.8)(35)$	$(1.8)(15)(0.\overline{7})$

√8.

A particular rent price increased x% from 2003 to 2004
The rent then decreased by x% from 2004 to 2005
x is a positive integer

Quantity A	**Quantity B**
The difference between 2004's price and 2003's price, in dollars.	The difference between 2004's price and 2005's price in dollars.

✗ 9.

$$m = 120\% \text{ of } n$$

Quantity A	**Quantity B**
$\dfrac{6}{5}n$	$\dfrac{5}{6}m$

✗10.

Quantity A	**Quantity B**
$0.125 + \dfrac{4}{5} + \dfrac{2}{3} + 1.2$	$0.8 + 0.\overline{6} + \dfrac{6}{5} + \dfrac{1}{8}$

Answer Key

1. A   2. A   3. B   4. C   5. B   6. B   7. A   8. B   9. D   10. C

Solutions

1. **A:** The common information tells us that the 2006 population rose by 40% to a population of 10,080. If x is the population in 2006, then written as math, that's $1.4x = 10,080$.

WARNING: You may NOT simply take away 40% of 10,080. This will yield an incorrect answer. Why? The 40% increase is 40% *of the 2006 population,* not 40% of the 2007 population. To calculate that, you need the equation $1.4x = 10,080$.

So, $x = \dfrac{10,080}{1.4} = 7,200$, which is greater than 7,000.

Alternatively, we could use Quantity B as a benchmark.

What if the original population had been 7,000? Let's raise THAT by 40%. One fast way to increase by 40% is to multiply by 1.4, rather than multiplying by 0.4 to generate the 40% and then adding it back on to the original number.

$$\begin{array}{r} 1.4 \\ \times\, 7{,}000 \\ \hline 9{,}800.0 \end{array}$$

That is, if the 2006 population had been 7,000, the 2007 population would have been 9,800. Since the population was actually 10,080, we know that the original population must have been higher than 7,000.

The answer is A.

2. **A:** Compare, Don't Calculate. It is not necessary to "solve" this problem, just to note that $\dfrac{1}{3}+\dfrac{1}{4}+\dfrac{7}{12}$ is more than

1. How do we know that? Well, $\dfrac{7}{12}$ is more than half already. $\dfrac{1}{4}+\dfrac{1}{4}$ would be another half, and $\dfrac{1}{3}$ is more than $\dfrac{1}{4}$.

Thus, is $\dfrac{1}{3}+\dfrac{1}{4}$ more than half.

In Quantity A, "more than half" plus "more than half" is "more than 1."
In Quantity B, dividing 1 by "more than 1" is "less than 1."

The answer is A.

3. **B:** This is another Compare, Don't Calculate problem. Since $\dfrac{1}{6}$ is present on both sides, simply subtract it.

Quantity A	**Quantity B**
$\dfrac{1}{6} - \left(\dfrac{1}{2}\right)^2 + \left(-\dfrac{1}{4}\right)^2$	$\dfrac{1}{6}$
$-\left(\dfrac{1}{2}\right)^2 + \left(-\dfrac{1}{4}\right)^2$	0

Now you only have to determine whether $-\left(\dfrac{1}{2}\right)^2 + \left(-\dfrac{1}{4}\right)^2$ is negative, positive, or zero.

$$-\left(\dfrac{1}{2}\right)^2 + \left(-\dfrac{1}{4}\right)^2 =$$
$$-\dfrac{1}{4} + \dfrac{1}{16}$$

Since $-\dfrac{1}{4} + \dfrac{1}{16}$ is definitely still negative, no further calculation is needed.

The answer is B.

4. **C:** The calculator might be tempting here, but there's a faster way. These columns can both be simplified quickly if we split the numerator of each fraction.

Quantity A	**Quantity B**
$\dfrac{\dfrac{4}{3} + (-2)}{-2} =$	$\dfrac{-\dfrac{4}{3} + 2}{2} =$
$\dfrac{\dfrac{4}{3}}{-2} + \dfrac{-2}{-2}$	$\dfrac{\dfrac{-4}{3}}{2} + \dfrac{2}{2}$

Since $-2/-2$ and $2/2$ are each equal to 1, cancel them out from each side.

Quantity A	**Quantity B**
$\dfrac{\dfrac{4}{3}}{-2}$	$\dfrac{\dfrac{4}{3}}{-2}$

On both sides, we have $\dfrac{4}{3}$ divided by 2, with a single negative sign. When working with fractions, it doesn't matter whether a negative sign is with the numerator, with the denominator, or "out front"—for example, $\dfrac{-1}{2}$, $\dfrac{1}{-2}$, and $-\dfrac{1}{2}$ are all equal. Don't bother to simplify either column.

The answer is C.

5. B: This is another problem for which we can split the numerator of each fraction.

Quantity A	$x > 1$	**Quantity B**
$\dfrac{x+5}{x} = \dfrac{x}{x} + \dfrac{5}{x}$		$\dfrac{(x-1)+5}{x-1} = \dfrac{x-1}{x-1} + \dfrac{5}{x-1}$

Since $\dfrac{x}{x}$ and $\dfrac{x-1}{x-1}$ are each equal to 1, cancel them out from both sides.

Quantity A	**Quantity B**
$\dfrac{5}{x}$	$\dfrac{5}{x-1}$

We know x is a positive number greater than 1. So, remember: *as the denominator gets larger, the fraction gets smaller.* Thus, Quantity B, which has the smaller denominator, is the larger fraction. The answer is B.

6. B: We are told that $x = -y$ and that neither one is zero; that is, the two numbers are inverses of one another (such as 2 and -2). However, when both are squared, the negative one becomes positive and the two values become equal. $x^2 = y^2$, so we can simply divide x^2 and y^2 out to get:

Quantity A	**Quantity B**
$\dfrac{5.5}{5}$	$\dfrac{3}{2.5}$

Although the fractions have different denominators, we can very easily convert to a common denominator of 5. Multiply the fraction in Quantity B by $\dfrac{2}{2}$.

Quantity A	**Quantity B**
$\dfrac{5.5}{5}$	$\dfrac{3}{2.5} \times \dfrac{2}{2} = \dfrac{6}{5}$

The fraction in Quantity B is larger.

7. A: First, divide the common element $(0.\overline{7})$ from each side to get:

Quantity A	**Quantity B**
$(0.8)(35)$	$(1.8)(15)$

Now, it's a calculator workout.

$(0.8)(35) = 28$
$(1.8)(15) = 27$

The answer is A.

8. B: An important consideration in dealing with percents is the size of the total. We don't know 2003's rent price, but we do know that 2004's—after the increase—is higher.

When the rent increases from 2003 to 2004, it goes up *x% of 2003's price.*
When the rent decreases from 2004 to 2005, it goes down *x% of 2004's price.*

Since 2004's price is higher than 2003's price, the second change is a greater dollar figure. That is, both changes are *x*%, but the second change is *x*% of a larger number, and hence a larger change in dollars. Quantity B's figure is larger.

You could also demonstrate this with numbers. Say 2003's price is $100 and *x* = 10. Thus:

$$2003 = \$100$$
$$2004 = \$110$$
$$2005 = \$99$$

The difference between 2004 and 2005 is greater than the difference between 2004 and 2003.

The answer is B.

9. D: Converting 120% to fraction form will help simplify. 120% is equivalent to $\frac{6}{5}$. Rewrite the common

information as $m = \frac{6}{5}n$. Now substitute $\frac{6}{5}n$ in place of *m* in Quantity B.

Quantity A	**Quantity B**
$\frac{6}{5}n$	$\frac{5}{6}m = \frac{5}{6}\left(\frac{6}{5}n\right)$

Thus, Quantity A is equal to $\frac{6}{5}n$ and Quantity B is simply equal to n ($\frac{5}{6} \times \frac{6}{5} = 1$). It would seem that Quantity A is

larger—however, what if *n* is negative? For example, if *n* is −1, Quantity A would be −1.2 and Quantity B would be −1, making Quantity B larger.

The answer is D.

10. C: Use percent benchmarks to compare columns, and cancel common elements. (The repeating decimal should be a clue that you are not really required to add all those quantities).

$0.125 = \frac{1}{8}$, so cancel 0.125 from Quantity A and $\frac{1}{8}$ from Quantity B.

$\frac{4}{5} = 0.8$, so cancel $\frac{4}{5}$ from Quantity A and 0.8 from Quantity B.

$\frac{2}{3} = 0.\overline{6}$, so cancel $\frac{2}{3}$ from Quantity A and $0.\overline{6}$ from Quantity B.

The last remaining quantities, 1.2 and $\dfrac{6}{5}$, are also equal. The two columns are equal.

The answer is C.

Alternatively, use the calculator! One of the nice things about the on-screen calculator is that it respects order of operations. In other words, just key in the formula:

$$0.125 + 4 \div 5 + 2 \div 3 + 1.2 =$$

And you'll get 2.7917 for quantity A.

Now the same for B:

$$0.8 + 0.6667 + 6 \div 5 + 1 \div 8 =$$

And you'll get 2.7917.

The answer is C.

Chapter 5
of

QUANTITATIVE COMPARISONS &
DATA INTERPRETATION

GEOMETRY

In This Chapter . . .

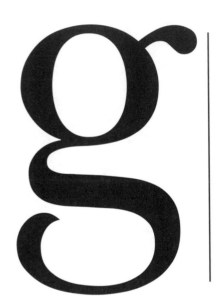

- Shape Geometry

- Variable Creation

- Word Geometry

- Using Numbers

GEOMETRY

This chapter is different from the others. The other topic chapters (Algebra, NPs, FDPs and WPs) are broken down into content areas (exponents, quadratic equations, etc.). This chapter provides a more general approach for Geometry questions, classified not by content area (e.g. Circles, Polygons), but by format.

Success on Geometry QC questions will still be largely determined by your knowledge of the rules and formulas associated with all the shapes tested on the GRE. This chapter offers a practical approach to correctly applying these rules and formulas to EVERY QC question, regardless of the shape or shapes being tested.

This chapter is broken down as follows:

    1)   How to deal with **Shape Geometry** questions, which include a **diagram**.

          A.   What to do when Quantity B contains a **number**.
          B.   What to do when Quantity B contains an **unknown**, such as a variable or an angle shown in the diagram.

    2)   How to deal with **Word Geometry** questions, which do *not* include a diagram.

Throughout the chapter we will emphasize a common theme: a 3-step process for tackling Geometry QC questions.

    1) Establish What You NEED TO KNOW
    2) Establish What You KNOW
    3) Establish What You DON'T KNOW

Shape Geometry

A. Quantity B is a NUMBER

The most straightforward QC Geometry problems are ones in which you are given the diagram and Quantity B is a number. We can attack these with the basic process. In most cases, you should quickly redraw the diagram you are given. Avoid the temptation simply to "look and solve," since you could easily make mistakes.

On Geometry QCs, as on all QCs, there is always the possibility that you will not have enough information, resulting in a correct answer of D. However, to arrive at the correct answer consistently, you must *act as though there is enough information*, while accepting that *the answer may ultimately be D*.

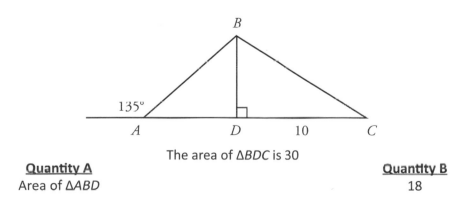

The area of △BDC is 30

Quantity A	**Quantity B**
Area of △ABD	18

For any Geometry QC problem, the first step is the same: Establish What You NEED TO KNOW.

Quantity B is a NUMBER, so no calculations are necessary.

Quantity A is the area of triangle *ABD*. This is the value you NEED TO KNOW. For any value you need to know, there are three possible scenarios:

      1) You can find an exact value.
      2) You can find a range of possible values.
      3) You do not have enough information to find the value.

Approach every Geometry QC as if you will be able to find an exact value, but recognize that you won't always be able to.

Now that you have established what you need to know, it is time to Establish What You KNOW.

To figure out what you know, use the given information to find values for previously unknown LENGTHS and ANGLES. You will do this by SETTING UP EQUATIONS and MAKING INFERENCES.

Keywords such as *area, perimeter* and *circumference* are good indications that you can set up equations to solve for a previously unknown LENGTH. In this example, the area of triangle *BDC* is given. First, write the general formula for area of a triangle, and then plug in all the known values.

$$\text{Area}_{\triangle BDC} = \frac{1}{2}(b)(h)$$

The area is given as 30, and line segment DC is the base of the triangle.

$$30 = \frac{1}{2}(10)(h)$$

Isolate *h* to solve for the height of the triangle.

$$30 = \frac{1}{2}(10)(h)$$

$$30 = 5h$$

$$6 = h$$

Immediately add any new information to your diagram.

*Manhattan*GRE*Prep
the new standard

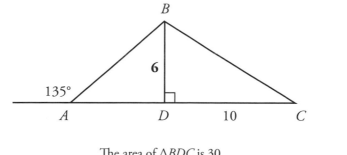

The area of △BDC is 30

Quantity A	**Quantity B**
Area of △ABD	18

Now that the length of *BD* is known, you can use the Pythagorean Theorem to calculate the length of *BC*.

$$(6)^2 + (10)^2 = (BC)^2$$
$$36 + 100 = (BC)^2$$
$$136 = (BC)^2$$
$$\sqrt{136} = BC$$

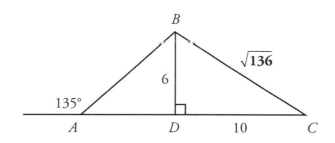

The area of △BDC is 30

Quantity A	**Quantity B**
Area of △ABD	18

At this stage, no other lengths can be calculated. Now ask yourself, "Are there any equations I can set up to find new angles?"

In general, you will find new angles with formulas that involve sums. Key features of diagrams include lines or intersecting lines with one known angle, parallel lines with a transversal and one known angle, and triangles with two known angles.

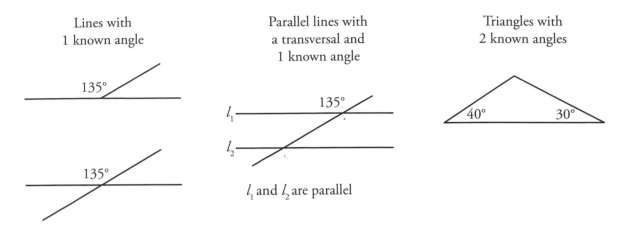

Lines with
1 known angle

Parallel lines with
a transversal and
1 known angle

Triangles with
2 known angles

l_1 and l_2 are parallel

In this diagram, we have a line with a known angle. Line segment *AB* divides the line into two parts. Straight lines have a degree measure of 180°, so set up an equation.

$$135° + \angle BAD = 180°$$
$$\angle BAD = 45°$$

Put 45° on your copy of the diagram. Use the calculator for this sort of computation if need be. Once you get fast, you should do the computation in your head, but you should always add it to the picture.

By the same logic, you also know that $\angle BDA = 90$.

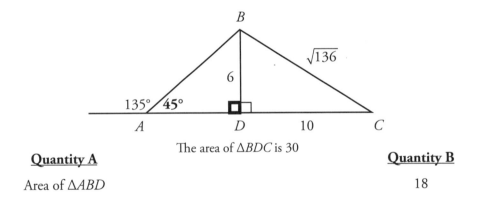

The area of $\triangle BDC$ is 30

Quantity A	**Quantity B**
Area of $\triangle ABD$	18

Now two of the angles in triangle *ABD* are known. You can solve for the third angle.

$$90° + 45° + \angle ABD = 180°$$
$$135° + \angle ABD = 180°$$
$$\angle ABD = 45°$$

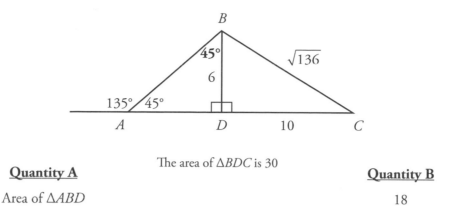

The area of △BDC is 30

Quantity A	**Quantity B**
Area of △ABD	18

At this stage, no more equations can be set up. Another important component when solving Geometry QC problems is MAKING INFERENCES. Not everything you learn will come from equations. Rather, special properties of shapes and relationships between shapes will allow you to make inferences.

In this diagram, ∠BAD and ∠ABD both lie in triangle ABD and have a degree measure of 45°. That means that triangle ABD is isosceles, and that the sides opposite ∠BAD and ∠ABD are equal. Side BD has a length of 6, which means side AD also has a length of 6.

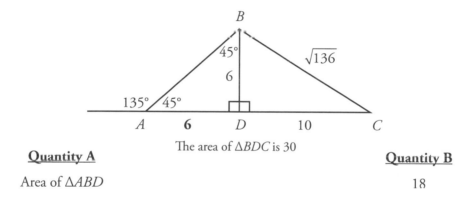

The area of △BDC is 30

Quantity A	**Quantity B**
Area of △ABD	18

Remember that the value you need to know is the area of triangle ABD. There is now sufficient information in the diagram to find that value. AD is the base and BD is the height.

$$\text{Area}_{\triangle ABD} = \frac{1}{2}(6)(6) = 18$$

The values in the two columns are equal and the answer is C.

You may have noticed that we did not need the length of BC ($\sqrt{136}$) in order to answer the question. So why did we calculate it?

We calculated it because at that stage of the problem, we were not sure whether we would need it. If you do not know yet how you will get the answer you need, then you should take the time to figure out everything you know. Once you have all the possible information, then you will have a better idea of how to use the information to answer the question.

In this instance, the length of *BC* was superfluous, but in general, you should feel comfortable finding missing values even if you are not sure why you need them. If nothing else, at least figure out that you *can* figure out the length of *BC*.

Problem Recap: Many QCs will provide enough information to reach a definite conclusion. To solve for the value you NEED TO KNOW:

Establish What You KNOW

> 1) SET UP EQUATIONS to find the values of previously unknown LINES and ANGLES.
> 2) MAKE INFERENCES to find additional information.

Establish What You DON'T KNOW

While many questions provide you enough information, you will not always be able to find an exact number for the value you need. For these questions, an additional step will be required: Establish What You DON'T KNOW.

Even though you will not always be able to find the exact value of something you NEED to know, implicit constraints within a diagram will often provide you a range of possible values. You will need to identify this range.

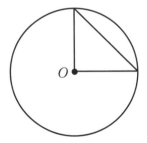

The circle with center *O*
has an area of 4π

Quantity A	**Quantity B**
Area of the triangle	1.5

First, establish what you NEED TO KNOW. To find the area of the triangle, you will need the base and the height.

Now, establish what you KNOW. The area of the circle is 4π, and Area $= \pi r^2$, so:

> $4\pi = \pi r^2$
> $4 = r^2$
> $2 = r$

The radius equals 2. Two lines in the diagram are radii. Label these radii.

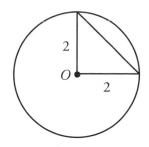

The circle with center O has
an area of 4π

Quantity A

Area of the triangle

Quantity B

1.5

Now the question becomes, "Is there enough information to find the area of the triangle?"

Be careful! Remember, DON'T TRUST THE PICTURE. The triangle in the diagram appears to be a right triangle. If that were the case, then the radii could act as the base and the height of the triangle, and the area would be:

$$\text{Area} = \frac{1}{2}(b)(h) = \frac{1}{2}(2)(2) = 2$$

The answer would be A. But there is one problem—the diagram does not provide any information about $\angle O$.

Of course, we do know a few things about the angle. Because $\angle O$ is one angle in a triangle, it has an implicit range: it must be greater than 0° and less than 180°.

$\angle O$ is a value you DON'T KNOW. The question now becomes, "How do changes to $\angle O$ affect the area of the triangle?" To find out, take the unknown value ($\angle O$) to EXTREMES.

We know what the area of the triangle is when $\angle O = 90°$. What happens as $\angle O$ increases?

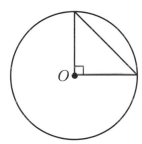 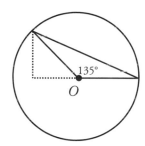 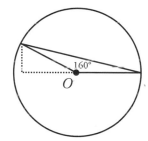

As $\angle O$ increases, the height of the triangle decreases, and thus the area of the triangle decreases as well.

In fact, as $\angle O$ gets closer and closer to its maximum value, the height gets closer and closer to 0. As the height gets closer to 0, so does the area of the triangle.

In other words:

$0 <$ area of triangle ≤ 2

Compare this range to Quantity B. The area of the triangle can be either greater than or less than 1.5. The correct answer is D.

Problem Recap: On some Geometry QC questions, it will be impossible to find an exact value for the value you need. After you have established what you NEED TO KNOW and established what you KNOW, you have to establish what you DON'T KNOW.

For values that you DON'T KNOW, take them to EXTREMES and see how changes affect the value you need to know.

B. Quantity B is an Unknown Value

This section is about some of the situations you will encounter when both columns contain UNKNOWN VALUES.

The basic process remains the same:

> Establish What You NEED TO KNOW
> Establish What You KNOW
> Establish What You DON'T KNOW

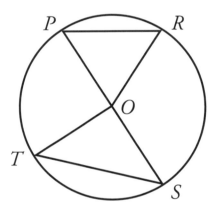

Quantity A		**Quantity B**
	O is the center of the circle	
	angle *POR* > angle *TOS*	
PR		*TS*

The first step, Establish What You NEED TO KNOW, is now more complicated, because there are two unknown values: Quantity A AND Quantity B.

When both columns contain an unknown, you need to know EITHER the values in both columns OR, more likely, the RELATIVE SIZE of the two values. For this problem, we will need to either solve for the values of *PR* and *TS* or determine their relative size.

Now, Establish What You KNOW. Remember: Don't Trust The Picture! The way the diagram is drawn, *TS*, appears larger than *PR*. That means nothing.

Actually, there is not a whole lot to know—no actual numbers have been given. *OP, OR, OT* and *OS* are radii, and thus have equal lengths. Other than that, the only thing we know is that ∠*POR* > ∠*TOS*.

the new standard

With no numbers provided in the question, finding exact values for either column is out of the question. But you may still be able to say something definite about their RELATIVE SIZE.

Now Establish What You DON'T KNOW. What values in the diagram are unknown and can affect the lengths of *PR* and *TS*? ∠*POR* and ∠*TOS* fulfill both criteria. Take the values of ∠*POR* and ∠*TOS* to EXTREMES.

How do changes to ∠*POR* and ∠*TOS* affect the lengths of *PR* and *TS*?

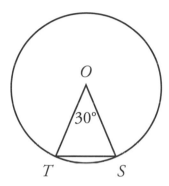 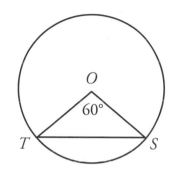 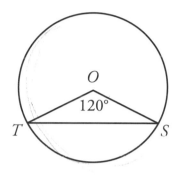

As ∠*TOS* gets bigger, so does *TS*. We can assume the same relationship is true in triangle *POR*.

Because *OP* = *OR* = *OT* = *OS*, we can directly compare the two triangles. ∠*POR* > ∠*TOS*, which means that no matter what the values of ∠*POR* and ∠*TOS* actually are, *PR* is definitely larger than *TS*. The correct answer is A.

Problem Recap: On questions for which both columns contain UNKNOWN VALUES, don't expect to find exact values for either column. Instead, look to gauge RELATIVE SIZE.

To judge relative size, establish what you DON'T KNOW and take those values to EXTREMES. Identify how changes to these unknown values change the values in the columns.

Variable Creation

Take a look at another example of a Geometry QC in which both columns are unknown values.

Quantity A	**Quantity B**
v	*w*

As in the preceding example, there are no numbers given, so an exact value for any of these angles is impossible to determine.

What you NEED TO KNOW is the relative size of *v* and *w*. As this type of problem gets more difficult, it becomes more difficult to establish what you KNOW.

An important feature of this diagram is that the intersection of the three lines creates a triangle. Triangles, when they appear, are often very important parts of diagrams, because there are many rules related to triangles that test makers can make use of. This question appears to be about angles. After all, the values in both columns are angles. CREATE VARIABLES to represent the three angles of the triangle.

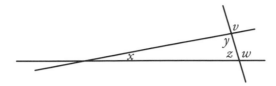

Part of the challenge is the fact that there are actually many relationships, and many equations you could create. For instance:

$$x + y + z = 180$$
$$w + z = 180$$

But not all of these relationships will help determine the relative size of v and w. You need to find relationships that will allow you to directly compare v and w.

The best bet for a link between v and w is the triangle in the center of the diagram. Try to express v and w in terms of x, y, and z.

Begin with v. Angles v and y are vertical angles, and thus equal. In Quantity A, replace v with y.

Quantity A	**Quantity B**
$v = y$	w

Now, if you can express w in terms of y, then you may be able to determine the relative size of v and w.

Based on the diagram, you know $w + z = 180$, so $w = 180 - z$.

Quantity A	**Quantity B**
y	$w = 180 - z$

You can't directly compare y and $(180 - z)$, so keep going. Try to find an equation that links y and z.

Remember we also know that $x + y + z = 180$. Isolate z.

$$x + y + z = 180$$
$$z = 180 - x - y$$

Now substitute $(180 - x - y)$ for z in Quantity B.

Quantity A	**Quantity B**
y	$180 - (180 - x - y) =$ $x + y$

Now we can directly compare the two columns. We know that x and y both represent angles, and so must be positive, so $x + y$ must be greater than y. The correct answer is B.

By the way, we've just proven that the exterior angle (w) is equal to the sum of the two remote interior angles ($x + y$). This is true in every case:

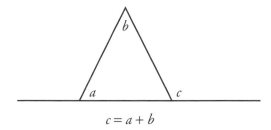

$$c = a + b$$

This is a good rule to know!

Problem Recap: One way that Geometry QC questions get harder is that the relationship between the two columns (when both columns contain UNKNOWN VALUES) becomes harder to identify.

If a diagram presents a common shape, such as a triangle or a quadrilateral, it is often helpful to CREATE VARIABLES to represent unknown angles or lengths. Use the properties of the shapes to create equations and express both columns in terms of the same variables.

Word Geometry

This section is devoted to QC questions that test your knowledge of Geometry, but don't provide a picture.

4 points, *P, Q, R* and *T* lie in a
plane. *PQ* is parallel to *RT* and
PR = QT

Quantity A	**Quantity B**
PQ	RT

The basic process remains the same. First, Establish What You NEED TO KNOW.

Both columns contain unknown values, so you need to determine the RELATIVE SIZE of each line segment.

Now, Establish What You KNOW. For ANY Word Geometry question, the first thing you need to do is DRAW THE PICTURE.

You want to draw a picture that is accurate, but quick. And remember, you can always redraw the figure if you run into trouble.

For this question, the easiest way to start is to draw the parallel lines.

_____

_____

You know that points *P* & *Q* lie on one line, and *R* & *T* lie on the other, but you don't know their relative sizes. But you do know that *PR = QT*.

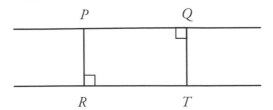

To start, the easiest thing to do is align the points so that they form a rectangle. Now, $PR = QT$. This diagram reflects all the information provided.

Now, take another look at the columns.

Quantity A	**Quantity B**
PQ	RT

According to the diagram, $PQ = RT$.   A̶B̶CD

You're not done. You need to TRY TO PROVE D.

Now the final step: Establish What You DON'T KNOW. Remember that the diagram above is only one possible way to represent the common information. Ask yourself, "What can change in this diagram?"

In the diagram above, PQ and RT were drawn perpendicular to the two parallel lines. But the angle can change. Redraw the diagram with PR and QT slanted.

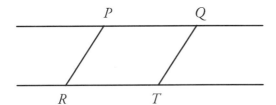

This diagram represents another possible configuration of the four points. Now how does PQ compare to RT?

Although it may not be immediately obvious, PQ is still equal to RT. Whereas the first diagram created a rectangle, this diagram has created a parallelogram. For additional practice, prove that $PQRT$ is a parallelogram.

It may be tempting to choose C at this stage. But be careful! The key to Word Geometry questions is to avoid making ANY assumptions not explicitly stated in the common information.

It is not sufficient to merely change the diagram. Ask yourself, "What can I change in the diagram to change the relative size of PQ and RT?"

Changing the angle at which segments PR and QT intersected the parallel lines was not sufficient to achieve different results. What else can change?

The two diagrams above share a common feature that is not required by the common information: PR and QT are parallel.

Redraw the figure so that PR and QT are NOT parallel, but still equal.

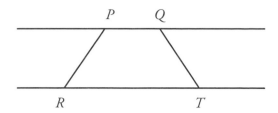

In this version of the diagram, *RT* is clearly longer than *PQ*. The answer is D.

Problem Recap: Word Geometry problems follow the same basic process. The values in both columns were unknown values, so you NEEDED TO KNOW the RELATIVE SIZE of the line segments in question.

For ANY Word Geometry question, the first step in Establishing What You KNOW is the same: DRAW THE PICTURE. Note that it will sometimes be necessary to redraw the picture if you need to PROVE D.

As you establish what you DON'T KNOW, try to determine what about your diagram can change, and always ask, "What can change that will affect the relative size of the values in the columns?" In this particular question, you needed to test situations in which *PR* and *QT* were both parallel and not parallel to answer the question correctly.

Using Numbers

For many Word Geometry QC questions, USING NUMBERS is an effective technique.

This technique is most effective when the question references specific dimensions of a shape (e.g. length, width, radius) but provides no actual numbers.

Rectangles *R* and *S* have equal
areas. Rectangle *R*'s length is
greater than Rectangle *S*'s width.

Quantity A	**Quantity B**
The area of Rectangle *R* if	The area of Rectangle *S* if
the length increases 30%	the width increases 30%

First, Establish What You NEED TO KNOW. Both columns have an unknown value, so you will have to judge their RELATIVE SIZE.

The best way to judge the relative size of each column is to USE NUMBERS.

The common information states the rectangles have equal areas. An easy number to use for the area is 10. The numbers chosen in this example are only one set of possibilities, but they were chosen because they are easy to use.

$$\text{Area}_R = \text{Area}_S = 10$$

Now DRAW THE PICTURE. Make sure you include the numbers you chose.

Each rectangle has an area of 10, but the length of *R* is greater than the width of *S*.

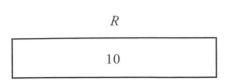

Quantity A mentions the length of *R* and Quantity B mentions the width of *S*. Pick values for the length and width of *R* and *S*.

Make the length of *R* 10 and the width 1. Make the length of *S* 2 and the width 5.

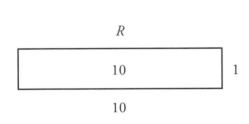

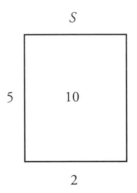

Quantity A	**Quantity B**
The area of Rectangle *R* if	The area of Rectangle *S* if
the length increases 30%	the width increases 30%

Now evaluate the columns. Start with Quantity A. Increase the length of *R* by 30%.

130% of 10 is $(1.3)(10) = 13$

The new area of *R* is $l \times w = (13)(1) = 13$.

Quantity A   **Quantity B**

R

| 13 | 1 |

13

                                                                    The area of Rectangle *S* if
                                                                    the width increases 30%

Now evaluate Quantity B. Increase the width of *S* by 30%.

130% of 5 is $(1.3)(5) = 6.5$

Use the calculator for this computation if need be.

*Manhattan*GRE*Prep*
the new standard

The new area of S is $l \times w = (2)(6.5) = 13$.

Quantity A	**Quantity B**
R	S

Quantity A:
$$\boxed{\quad\quad 13 \quad\quad}\; 1$$
$$13$$

Quantity B:
$$6.5 \;\boxed{\; 13 \;}$$
$$2$$

The new areas are equal. This result will hold regardless of the precise length you choose. The correct answer is C.

Problem Recap: USING NUMBERS is a useful strategy when a Word Geometry Question references specific dimensions of shapes (e.g. length, width, radius) but does not provide any actual numbers. As long as you pick numbers that match any restrictions in the common information or columns, the conclusion you arrive at will be valid and lead to the correct answer.

Problem Set

1.

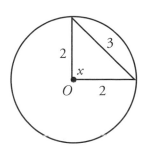

O is the center of the circle

Quantity A		Quantity B
The degree measure of angle *x*	C	90°

2.

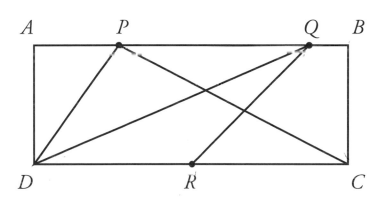

ABCD is a rectangle
R is the midpoint of DC

Quantity A   Quantity B
The area of triangle DPC   Twice the area of triangle DQR

3.   The circumference of Circle A is twice the circumference of Circle B

Quantity A   Quantity B
The area of Circle A   Twice the area of Circle B

4.   1,600 feet of fencing is used to fence off a square plot

<u>Quantity A</u>   <u>Quantity B</u>

The plot's new area if the length were reduced   The plot's new area if the length were equal to 398
by 4 feet and the height increased by 4 feet.   feet and the width were equal to 402 feet.

5.

<u>Quantity A</u>   <u>Quantity B</u>

The third side of an isosceles triangle   The third side of an isosceles triangle
with sides of 3 and 9   with sides of 6 and 8

6.

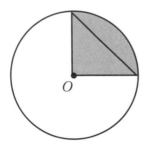

The area of the circle is 16π
The area of the shaded region $< 4\pi$

<u>Quantity A</u>   <u>Quantity B</u>

The degree measure of angle O 90

7.   A circle with radius $\dfrac{4}{\sqrt{\pi}}$ has the same area as a particular square

<u>Quantity A</u>   <u>Quantity B</u>

9π The square's area if each side were
increased by 1

8.

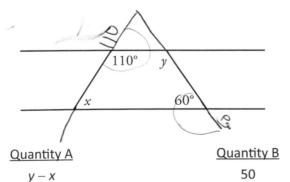

<u>Quantity A</u>   <u>Quantity B</u>

$y - x$ 50

9.   Rectangle A has twice the area of Rectangle B and less than 1/2 the width

Quantity B   Quantity B

Rectangle A's area   Rectangle B's area if its width is
                                             increased by more than 2

10. l_1 and l_2 are parallel lines.

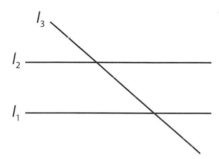

Quantity A   Quantity B
The slope of line l_1 The slope of line l_2
minus the slope of l_3 minus the slope of l_3

Answer Key

1. A   2. C   3. A   4. B   5. A   6. B   7. A   8. D   9. D   10. C

Solutions

1. **A:** Let's Use Quantity B as a benchmark by trying to make x equal to 90. That is, we will try to prove C. If it doesn't work, we'll have our answer. Mark the angle as 90 and use the Pythagorean Theorem to find the hypotenuse, using the two legs of 2:

$$2^2 + 2^2 = (c)^2$$
$$c^2 = 8$$
$$c = \sqrt{8}$$
$$c = 2\sqrt{2}$$

However, we know that the hypotenuse is actually 3, not $2\sqrt{2}$. The bigger the hypotenuse, the bigger angle x is going to be (picture how the triangle "opens" as x increases). Since $\sqrt{2}$ is about 1.4, $2\sqrt{2}$ is about 2.8. If angle x were 90, the hypotenuse would be about 2.8. However, the hypotenuse is actually 3, so angle x must be bigger than 90.

The answer is A.

2. **C:** There are no numbers mentioned anywhere in the problem, but that doesn't mean the answer is D. Some important observations: both of the triangles mentioned in the columns have the same height (whatever the rectangle's height is). Also, since R is the midpoint of DC, triangle DPC's base is exactly twice the length of triangle DQR's base.

Use numbers to make the comparison easier. Let the height of each triangle (also the height of the rectangle) be 5. Let the base of triangle DPC be 8 and the base of triangle DQR be 4.

Quantity A	**Quantity B**
The area of triangle DPC =	Twice the area of triangle DQR =
$\frac{1}{2}(8)(5) = \mathbf{20}$	$2 \times \frac{1}{2}(4)(5) = \mathbf{20}$

Thus, the two columns are equal.

The answer is C.

3. **A:** Since the formula for circumference is simply $C = 2\pi r$, doubling the radius will double the circumference (this is NOT true for the area formula, which involves *squaring* the radius). Thus, from the common information "The circumference of Circle A is twice the circumference of Circle B," we can infer that the radius of A is twice that of B. For instance, let's say A's radius is 2 and B's radius is 1.

In that case, Quantity A = 4π. The area of circle B is π, so Quantity B = 2π. Quantity A is bigger.

This will work for any numbers you decide to use. If a circle's radius is double another circle's radius, its area will be four times as big, because the double-radius is then being squared. The answer is A.

*Manhattan*GRE Prep

4. B: A square has a perimeter of 1,600 feet. To find the length of each side of the square, divide 1,600 by 4, because each side has the same length. The length of each side of the square is 400.

Quantity A asks us about a 396 by 404 rectangle, and Quantity B asks us about a 398 by 402 rectangle. Using the calculator, we get 396 × 404 = 159,984 for quantity A and 398 × 402 = 159,996 for quantity B.

The answer is B.

Notice that if two numbers have a finite sum (396 + 404 = 800 and 398 + 402 = 800), their product will get larger as the two numbers get closer together. For example, 4 × 4 is greater than 3 × 5, 99 × 101 is greater than 97 × 103, and so on and so forth for any similar example you can think of.

5. A: This is a question about the Third Side Rule, which says that the third side of a triangle must be less than the sum of the other two sides and greater than their difference. The triangle referenced in Quantity A has two sides of 3 and 9. By the Third Side Rule, the third side must be between 6 and 12 (the difference and the sum of 3 and 9). Since the triangle is isosceles and two sides must be of equal measure, the third side must be 9. (Also, try picturing a 3–3–9 triangle—it's impossible because the sides would never meet.)

The triangle referenced in Quantity B has two sides of 6 and 8. By the Third Side Rule, the third side must be between 2 and 14. Therefore, the third side could be either 6 or 8. However, although we don't know which of those values the third side actually is, we still have enough information to determine that Quantity B's value (either 6 or 8) is smaller than Quantity A's value, which is 9.

The answer is A.

6. B: Use Quantity B as a Benchmark. If the angle at O were equal to 90, the shaded region would have an area equal to $\frac{1}{4}$ that of the entire circle (since 90 is $\frac{1}{4}$ of 360). Thus, if the angle were equal to 90, the shaded region would have an area of 4π ($\frac{1}{4}$ of the entire circle's area). Since the area of the shaded region is actually less than 4π, the angle at O must be less than 90.

The answer is B.

7. A: A circle's radius is $\frac{4}{\sqrt{\pi}}$ and its area equals the square's area. Plug $\frac{4}{\sqrt{\pi}}$ into the formula for area of a circle:

$$A = \pi\left(\frac{4}{\sqrt{\pi}}\right)^2$$
$$A = \pi\left(\frac{16}{\pi}\right)$$
$$A = 16$$

Thus, the square's area is also 16 and the side is 4.

Quantity A is simply equal to 9π. Quantity B is the square's area if each side were increased by 1—that is, if each side were now equal to 5. Thus, Quantity B = 25. Since π is more than 3, Quantity A is more than 27.

The answer is A.

8. **D:** Note that we are NOT told that the two horizontal-seeming lines in the figure are actually parallel, so you may NOT assume this. We do know that all four angles of the quadrilateral must sum to 360, so we can deduce that $x + y$ must equal 190.

However, without knowing that we have parallel lines, we have no way of knowing how to "split up" the 190 between x and y, and therefore no way to know whether $y - x$ is greater than 50. (For instance, if the lines were parallel, y would equal 120 and x would equal 70, and $y - x$ would be exactly 50. Adjust the figure even one degree—for instance, if y gets larger, x will get proportionately smaller—and $y - x$ will no longer equal 50).

The answer is D.

9. **D:** Rectangle A has twice the area of Rectangle B and less than 1/2 the width. Start by drawing one scenario of how this could be:

Rectangle A

Rectangle B

40

5

1

4

Now, *Try to Prove D.*

In this scenario, Quantity A equals 40.

In Quantity B, Rectangle B's width is increased by "more than 2." (We should have a good clue here that, in mixing actual numbers with relative sizes, we're likely to be able to achieve a variety of results—a strong indicator of a D answer).

Therefore, the new width could be, for example, 8, or it could be 100. If the new width is 8, the new area would be 40, which would be equal to quantity A. If the new width is 100, the new area would be 500, way more than quantity A.

The answer is D.

10. **C:** This one's quick—this question is simply a test of the fact that parallel lines have equal slopes. Therefore, the slope of line l_1 and the slope of line l_2 are identical, and Quantities A and B are equal, regardless of the slope of line l_3.

The answer is C.

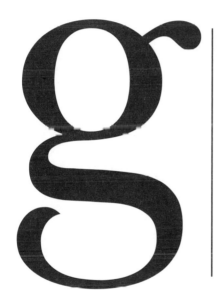

Chapter 6
of
QUANTITATIVE COMPARISONS &
DATA INTERPRETATION

NUMBER
PROPERTIES

In This Chapter . . .

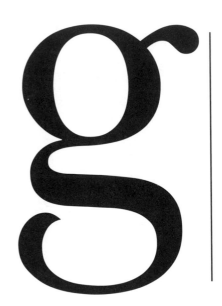

- Positives & Negatives
- Exponents
- Consecutive Integers

NUMBER PROPERTIES

Number Properties turns out to be very fertile ground for Quantitative Comparison questions. By creating situations that hinge on the general behavior of negative numbers or of fractions raised to an exponent, ETS can create conceptually challenging problems that do not require a lot of calculation. A very popular theme related to Number Properties is TRYING TO PROVE D.

Positives & Negatives

Perhaps no dichotomy is as important to Quantitative Comparisons as is the Positive / Negative distinction. For one thing, ETS can easily create a question about positives and negatives without having to use either word. But there are common clues. If you see any of the following clues in a Quantitative Comparison, ask yourself whether positive and negative numbers play a role.

1) Common information states that a variable is either greater than or less than 0.
   $x < 0$ → x is negative
   $y > 0$ → y is positive

2) The product of more than one variable is greater than or less than 0.
   $pq > 0$ → p and q have the same sign; they are either both positive or both negative

3) An expression that contains both a negative sign and an exponent.
   $(-x)^4$ → $(-x)^4$ is positive, since 4 is even

Greater than or Less than 0

These clues often mean that you can save time by making generalizations based on the signs of variables.

$x < 0$

<u>Quantity A</u>	<u>Quantity B</u>
$x - 2$	$-(x - 2)$

We want to not only get this question right, but we want to get it right **quickly**. One option is to plug in numbers for x.

For instance, plug in −1 for x.

$x < 0$

<u>Quantity A</u>	<u>Quantity B</u>
$(-1) - 2 = -3$	$-((-1) - 2) = 3$

When $x = -1$, Quantity B is bigger.   ~~A~~B~~C~~D

But do we know Quantity B will ALWAYS be bigger? No, we would need to try other numbers for x, and that will be time-consuming.

Instead, see whether you can MAKE A GENERALIZATION about the sign of each column. If x is negative, can we say anything definite about the sign of $x - 2$? Yes, we can. A negative minus a positive will always be negative.

We can rewrite Quantity A.

$$x < 0$$

Quantity A	**Quantity B**
NEGATIVE	$-(x - 2)$

Now we need to see whether we can make a generalization about Quantity B. Let's start with the expression inside the parentheses: $x - 2$. We know that $x - 2$ is always negative, so we can rewrite the expression as:

$- (\text{NEGATIVE})$

What we have is a negative number inside the parentheses being multiplied by a negative.

$(x - 2)$ is negative, so $-(x - 2)$ is positive.

We can rewrite Quantity B.

$$x < 0$$

Quantity A	**Quantity B**
NEGATIVE	POSITIVE

Instead of trying specific numbers, we made generalizations about the sign of each column. ANY positive number is greater than ANY negative number, so Quantity B will ALWAYS be greater. The correct answer is B.

Problem Recap: If you are told the sign of a variable (e.g. $x < 0$), try to MAKE A GENERALIZATION about the sign of each column.

Product of Variables Greater than or Less than 0

In the last problem, we knew the sign of the variable. That will not always be the case.

$$xy > 0$$

Quantity A	**Quantity B**
$x + y$	0

This question is still about positives and negatives, but now it concerns the signs of both x and y. The common information is telling us something very important. There are two possible scenarios:

    1) x and y are BOTH positive
    2) x and y are BOTH negative

To find our answer, we need to test both scenarios. As in the last problem, we are testing NOT with specific numbers, but with the signs of the variables.

Let's test the first scenario: x and y are both positive.

$$xy > 0$$

Quantity A	**Quantity B**
$x + y$	0

POSITIVE + POSITIVE =

POSITIVE

Quantity A will always be positive, regardless of the values of x and y.   A̶B̶C̶D

Now test the second scenario: x and y are both negative.

$$xy > 0$$

Quantity A	**Quantity B**
$x + y$	0

NEGATIVE + NEGATIVE =

NEGATIVE

Quantity A will always be negative, regardless of the values of x and y. The correct answer is D.

Problem Recap: When the product of more than one variable is either greater or less than 0, consider all possible signs and test all possible scenarios.

If $xy > 0$, the two scenarios are:

> 1) x and y are BOTH positive
> 2) x and y are BOTH negative

If $xy < 0$, the two scenarios are:

> 1) x is positive and y is negative
> 2) x is negative and y is positive

You will have to test BOTH scenarios to get the right answer consistently.

Exponents & Negatives

Another sign that you are dealing with positives and negatives is the combination of exponents and negative signs.

n is an integer

Quantity A	**Quantity B**
$(-3)^{2n}$	$(-3)^{2n + 1}$

When negative numbers are raised to a power, they follow a pattern:

> 1) Negative numbers raised to odd powers are negative
> 2) Negative numbers raised to even powers are positive

We need to see if we can MAKE A GENERALIZATION about the sign of each column. Let's start with Quantity A. n is an integer, so $2n$ will always be even. The exponent will always be even, and a negative raised to an even power will always be positive.

n is an integer

Quantity A	**Quantity B**
(NEGATIVE)^{EVEN} =	$(-3)^{2n+1}$
POSITIVE	

Now test Quantity B. $2n$ is always even, which means $2n + 1$ will always be odd. A negative number raised to an odd power is negative.

n is an integer

Quantity A	**Quantity B**
(NEGATIVE)^{EVEN} =	(NEGATIVE)^{ODD} =
POSITIVE	NEGATIVE

The correct answer is A.

Problem Recap: When problems contain both exponents and negative signs, try to make generalizations about the sign of each column.

> 1) A negative number raised to an ODD power is NEGATIVE
> 2) A negative number raised to an EVEN power is POSITIVE

Section Recap:

All of these problems have one thing in common: we can save time by figuring out whether each column is positive or negative.

Be on the lookout for these clues:

> 1) Common information states that a variable is greater or less than 0 (e.g. $x > 0$, $p < 0$)
> 2) Common information states the product of two variables is greater or less than 0 (e.g. $xy < 0$)
> 3) An expression contains both an exponent and a negative sign (e.g. $(-2)^x$)

Exponents

The test-makers love the following exponent rules:

> 1) Numbers greater than 1 get BIGGER as you raise them to higher powers
>
> $2^1 < 2^2 < 2^3$
> $2 < 4 < 8$

2) Numbers between 0 and 1 get SMALLER as you raise them to higher powers

$$\left(\frac{1}{2}\right)^1 > \left(\frac{1}{2}\right)^2 > \left(\frac{1}{2}\right)^3$$

$$\frac{1}{2} > \frac{1}{4} > \frac{1}{8}$$

When you see variables raised to exponents, don't forget about proper fractions (numbers between 0 and 1)!

Be on the lookout for questions that involve exponents and either fractions or variables that can be fractions.

x and *y* are positive

Quantity A	**Quantity B**
xy	$(xy)^2$

At first, this question may seem to be about positives and negatives. But if *x* and *y* are both positive, both columns will be positive. We cannot make a quick comparison using positives and negatives.

The key to this question is the exponent. We have the same combination of variables raised to different powers.

x and *y* are positive

Quantity A	**Quantity B**
$(xy)^1$	$(xy)^2$

First, try numbers greater than 1 for *x* and *y*. Plug in 2 for *x* and 3 for *y*.

x and *y* are positive

Quantity A	**Quantity B**
$(2)(3) = \mathbf{6}$	$((2)(3))^2 = 6^2 = \mathbf{36}$

In this case, Quantity B is bigger.   ~~AB~~C~~D~~

Don't stop there. We need to try to PROVE D. The common information did not tell us that *x* and *y* are integers – we should see what happens if they are fractions.

Plug in $\dfrac{1}{2}$ for *x* and $\dfrac{1}{3}$ for *y*.

x and *y* are positive

Quantity A	**Quantity B**
$\left(\dfrac{1}{2}\right)\left(\dfrac{1}{3}\right) = \dfrac{\mathbf{1}}{\mathbf{6}}$	$\left(\left(\dfrac{1}{2}\right)\left(\dfrac{1}{3}\right)\right)^2 = \left(\dfrac{1}{6}\right)^2 = \dfrac{\mathbf{1}}{\mathbf{36}}$

Fractions get smaller as they are raised to higher powers, so now Quantity A is larger than Quantity B. The correct answer is D.

Consecutive Integers

QC questions will sometimes ask you to compare the sum or product of sets of consecutive integers. The trick is to avoid finding the actual sums or products by ELIMINATING OVERLAP.

Quantity A	**Quantity B**
The product of all the integers from 2 to 23, inclusive	The product of all the integers from 5 to 24, inclusive

Both of these products are far too large to calculate in a reasonable amount of time, even with a calculator. Instead, we need to figure out which numbers appear in both products, and cancel those numbers.

In this problem, the numbers 5 through 23 appear in both sets. We can rewrite the products as:

Quantity A	**Quantity B**
$2 \times 3 \times 4 \times (5 \times 6 \times \ldots 22 \times 23)$	$(5 \times 6 \times \ldots 22 \times 23) \times 24$

The product of the numbers 5 through 23 is positive, and has the same value in each column. Therefore, because of the INVISIBLE INEQUALITY, we can divide out $(5 \times 6 \times \ldots 22 \times 23)$, and focus on what is left.

Quantity A	**Quantity B**
$\dfrac{2 \times 3 \times 4 \times (5 \times 6 \times \ldots 22 \times 23)}{(5 \times 6 \times \ldots 22 \times 23)} =$	$\dfrac{(5 \times 6 \times \ldots 22 \times 23) \times 24}{(5 \times 6 \times \ldots 22 \times 23)} =$
$2 \times 3 \times 4 = 24$	24

The values in the two columns are equal. The correct answer is C.

Problem Set

1. x is an integer

Quantity A	Quantity B
$\dfrac{1}{100^x}$	$\dfrac{1}{99^x}$

2. n is an integer

Quantity A	Quantity B
$(-1)^{2n+1} \times (-1)^n$	$(1)^n$

3. $1 < 3x < 2$

Quantity A	Quantity B
x^5	x^7

4. $98 < x < 102$
                     $103 < y < 107$

Quantity A	Quantity B
$y - x$	$|y - x|$

5. $xyz < 0$

Quantity A	Quantity B
$x + y + z$	$2x + 2y + 2z$

6.

Quantity A	Quantity B
$(-101)^{102}$	$(-102)^{101}$

7.

$$n < -1$$

Quantity A	Quantity B
$n^2 \cdot n^4$	$(n^2)^4$

8.

Quantity A	Quantity B
The sum of the consecutive integers from −12 to 13	13

9.

$$\frac{x}{y} < 0$$
$$y > x$$

Quantity A	Quantity B
$y - x$	xy

10.

Quantity A	Quantity B
The sum of the consecutive integers from 2 to 15	34 less than the sum of the consecutive integers from 1 to 17

Answer Key

1. D   2. D   3. A   4. C   5. D   6. A   7. B   8. C   9. A   10. C

Solutions

1. **D:** This question might be trying to trick you into picking A (the "bigger-looking" number) or maybe reasoning that a bigger number under a fraction gets smaller, and therefore picking B. But, of course, the exponent changes things. The easiest way to approach this is simply to plug in small values for x and try to prove D. We know that x is an integer. Let's try some values for which it will be easy to calculate a value:

If $x = 1$, Quantity B is bigger ($\frac{1}{99} > \frac{1}{100}$).

If $x = 0$, the columns are equal (since any number to a power of 0 is equal to 1).

Stop here—the answer is D.

2. **D:** Note that -1 and 1, when raised to an integer power, have very limited possibilities. -1 raised to an even power is 1, and -1 raised to an odd power is -1, whereas 1 raised to a power is always 1. Therefore, this is really a problem about odds and evens. So plug in a small even number and a small odd number and try to prove D.

If $n = 2$, Quantity A is equal to $(-1)^5 \times (-1)^7$, which is -1, and Quantity B is equal to 1.

If $n = 3$, Quantity A is equal to $(-1)^7 \times (-1)^3$, which is 1, and Quantity B is equal to 1.

Stop here—the answer is D.

3. **A:** Before proceeding to Quantities A and B, simplify $1 < 3x < 2$ by dividing through by 3:

$$\frac{1}{3} < x < \frac{2}{3}$$

x is therefore between $\frac{1}{3}$ and $\frac{2}{3}$. More importantly, x is definitely between zero and 1, which means it gets smaller when multiplied by itself.

Therefore, x^5 is larger than x^7.

The answer is A.

(It would be possible to plug in a value between 1/3 and 2/3, such as 1/2, which would make Quantity A equal to $\frac{1}{32}$ and Quantity B equal to $\frac{1}{128}$. However, a number properties approach is far superior here—because we know that x will behave in a certain way due to its being a fraction between zero and 1, we are saved from having to calculate anything to the 7th power).

4. C: The presence of fairly large numbers in the common information is merely a distraction—the point is that y is definitely larger than x. Therefore, $y - x$ is positive. A positive number is the same as its own absolute value. Therefore, the answer is C.

5. D: Try to make generalizations about the signs of variables. If xyz is negative, then there are two possible scenarios: all three are negative, or one is negative and the other two are positive. To find our answer, we need to test both scenarios.

If all three are negative, then both Quantity A and Quantity B have negative values. Since we can factor the 2 out of Quantity B to get 2 $(x + y + z)$, Quantity B's value is therefore twice Quantity A's value—that is, Quantity B becomes *more negative* and is therefore smaller. Quantity A would be bigger.

But if one of the variables were negative and the other two were positive, we wouldn't have enough to know the sign of $x + y + z$ (remember, when *multiplying or dividing,* knowing the signs of what you are multiplying or dividing is enough to know the sign of the answer, but when adding or subtracting, you need to know the relative sizes of what you are adding or subtracting). For instance, if x, y, and z are -1, 3, and 4, then $x + y + z$ is positive, and $2x + 2y + 2z$ (Quantity B) would be bigger.

The answer is D.

6. A: A good sign that a problem can perhaps be solved with just positives and negatives is the presence of both exponents and negative signs. Using only positives and negatives, consider the problem as such:

Quantity A	**Quantity B**
(negative)^{even}	(negative)^{odd}

Thus, Quantity A is positive and Quantity B is negative.

The answer is A.

7. B: Use exponent rules to simplify the expressions in each column.

Quantity A	**Quantity B**
$n^2 \cdot n^4 = n^6$	$(n^2)^4 = n^8$

In both columns, n is raised to an even power, so both columns will be positive. Because $n < -1$, the absolute value of n will get bigger as n is raised to higher powers. Therefore, Quantity B will be larger.

8. C: If we were to write out the integers in Quantity A, we'd have $-12 + -11 + -10 \ldots + -1 + 0 + 1 \ldots + 10 + 11 + 12 + 13$.

Note that for every negative there is a corresponding positive value. For instance, -12 cancels with 12, -11 cancels with 11, and so on. When all the canceling is through, we're left with 13.

The answer is C.

9. **A:** The common information should be enough for us to know that this is a positive/negative question. If x/y is negative, then x and y have different signs. If $y > x$, then y must be positive and x negative. In Quantity A, we have a positive minus a negative—this will create a greater positive. In Quantity B, we have a negative times a positive, which is always negative.

The answer is A.

10. **C:** To compare the sums or products of sets of consecutive integers, eliminate overlap in order to make a direct comparison. Here we will abbreviate "the sum of the consecutive integers from 2 to 15" as $(2 + 3... + 15)$:

Quantity A	**Quantity B**
$(2 + 3 \ldots + 15)$	$1 + (2 + 3 \ldots + 15) + 16 +$ $17 - 34$

Now eliminate $(2 + 3 \ldots + 15)$ from both sides:

Quantity A	**Quantity B**
0	$1 + 16 + 17 - 34$

Since $1 + 16 + 17 - 34 = 0$, the answer is C.

Chapter 7

of

QUANTITATIVE COMPARISONS &
DATA INTERPRETATION

WORD

PROBLEMS

In This Chapter . . .

- Ratios
- Statistics

WORD PROBLEMS

Overview

Word Problems very much fit into the framework of avoiding excessive computation. Difficult Word Problems questions are often difficult because they describe situations that do not translate obviously into solvable equations.

But there is an added wrinkle—word problems do not automatically provide enough information to solve for the desired values.

Milo can core x apples in 10 minutes
and peel y potatoes in 20 minutes

Quantity A	**Quantity B**
The number of apples Milo can core in an hour	The number of potatoes Milo can peel in an hour

The rate at which Milo can core apples is x apples / 10 min, or $6x$ apples / hour. The rate at which Milo can peel potatoes is y potatoes / 20 min, or $3y$ potatoes / hour. So the comparison is really $6x$ vs. $3y$. But without more information, we have no way to compare these two values. The answer is D.

Problem Recap: Whenever you see a word problem on Quantitative Comparisons, make sure you have the information you need before doing any computation. If you don't have enough info, the answer is D.

Ratios

Don't confuse a ratio with actual numbers of objects. For instance, if we know that a store carries red shirts and white shirts in a 2 to 3 ratio, the store may have 5 total shirts (2 red and 3 white), 10 total shirts (4 red and 6 white), 500 total shirts (200 red and 300 white), etc. What we do know is that there are more reds than whites and that the total number of shirts must be a multiple of 5.

Adding real numbers of objects to a ratio isn't very helpful without some real numbers of objects to begin with. For example, if a store carries red shirts and white shirts in a 2 to 3 ratio, what effect does adding 3 red shirts have? Well, if the store had 5 total shirts (2 red and 3 white), adding 3 red shirts changes the ratio to 5 to 3 (5 red and 3 white). But if we started with 500 total shirts (200 red and 300 white), adding 3 red shirts doesn't change the ratio very much at all; it's now 203 to 300. Try an example:

A university contains French majors and Spanish majors
in a 5 to 7 ratio.

Quantity A	**Quantity B**
The number of French majors if 10 French majors transfer into the university and no other students leave, join, or change majors	The number of French majors if 3/7 of the Spanish majors switch to French

Let's Try to Prove D. Start by constructing two scenarios for "A university contains French majors and Spanish majors in a 5 to 7 ratio." For the first scenario, use the smallest possible values: 5 French majors and 7 Spanish majors. For the second scenario, use much larger (but still easy to work with) numbers: 500 French majors and 700 Spanish majors.

the new standard

Evaluate the first scenario. For the first scenario (5 French majors and 7 Spanish majors), Quantity A gives us 15

French majors (5 + 10 = 15). In Quantity B, 3 Spanish majors switch to French $\left(\frac{3}{7} \times 7 = 3\right)$, so there are 8 French majors (5 + 3 = 8). In this scenario, Quantity A is bigger.

Now evaluate the second scenario (500 French majors and 700 Spanish majors). Quantity A gives us 510 French

majors (500 + 10 = 510). In Quantity B, 300 Spanish majors switch to French $\left(\frac{3}{7} \times 700 = 300\right)$ so there are 800 total French majors. In this scenario, Quantity B is bigger. The correct answer is D.

Problem Recap: Remember that ratios provide you NO information about actual values. To Try to Prove D on a ratios problem, choose one scenario in which the actual values are the same values as the ratio and choose another scenario in which the numbers are much larger (but still pick numbers that are easy to work with).

Statistics

Aside from the standard average formula (which you should know VERY well), there is a property of averages that mixes very nicely with the Quantitative Comparison format.

A company has two divisions. Division A
has 105 employees and an average salary
of $60,000. Division B has 93 employees
and an average salary of $70,000.

Quantity A	**Quantity B**
The average salary of all the employees at the company	$65,000

A lot of unnecessary computation could go into answering this Quantitative Comparison. Notice that our benchmark value in Quantity B is exactly halfway between the average salaries of the two divisions. This is very convenient for us, because we can use the principle of weighted averages.

Suppose that instead of 198 employees (105 + 93), you have 6 employees: 3 people in each division. To simplify things we can say that everyone in Division A makes $60,000 and everyone in Division B makes $70,000.

The average salary for all 6 employees will be:

$$\frac{3(60,000) + 3(70,000)}{6} = 65,000$$

There are an equal number of people in each division, so the average salary is the average of 60,000 and 70,000.

Think of average salaries as a spectrum. There are three scenarios:

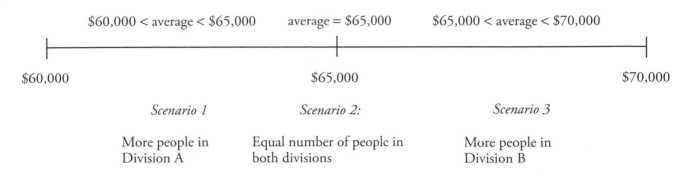

<table>
<tr><td>$60,000 < average < $65,000</td><td>average = $65,000</td><td>$65,000 < average < $70,000</td></tr>
</table>

| $60,000 | $65,000 | $70,000 |

| *Scenario 1* | *Scenario 2:* | *Scenario 3* |
| More people in Division A | Equal number of people in both divisions | More people in Division B |

The common information tells us there are more employees in Division A (105 vs. 93). The average salary of the whole company will be less than $65,000.

Quantity A	**Quantity B**
The average salary of all the employees at the company = **less than $65,000**	$65,000

The correct answer is B.

Problem Recap: In any question that involves two groups that have some kind of average value, use the principles of weighted averages.

If two groups have an equal number of members, the total average will be the average of the two groups

(ex. $\dfrac{3(60,000) + 3(70,000)}{6} = 65,000$).

If one group has more members, the total average will be closer to the average of that group

(ex. $\dfrac{105(60,000) + 93(70,000)}{198} = 64,696.97$). There's no need to do this calculation!

Problem Set

1.   Bag A contains red and black marbles in a 3 to 4 ratio   *9 to 10*
      Bag B contains red and black marbles in a 4 to 3 ratio   *10 to 9*

   Quantity A   **Quantity B**
   The total number of red marbles   *C*   The total number of black marbles
   in both bags combined   in both bags combined

2.   June can run 6 laps in *x* minutes   *24 laps = 4x*
                  Miriam can run 11 laps in 2*x* minutes   *11 laps = (2x)2*

   Quantity A   **Quantity B**
   The number of minutes it takes   *C*   The number of minutes it takes
   June to run 24 laps   Miriam to run 22 laps

3.   Abe's quiz scores are 62, 68, 74, and 68
               Ben's quiz scores are 66 and 70

   Quantity A   **Quantity B**
   The score Abe needs on his fifth   *A*   The score Ben needs on his third
   quiz to raise his average to 70   quiz to raise his average to 70

   78   *74*

4.   Set S = {2, 3, 5, 2, 11, 1}

   Quantity A   **Quantity B**
   The average of Set S   *C*   The mode of Set S if every
   4   number in the set were doubled
                                                4

5.   Silky Dark Chocolate is 80% cocoa
               Rich Milk Chocolate is 50% cocoa
               Smooth White Chocolate is 0% cocoa

   Quantity A   **Quantity B**
   Percent cocoa of a mixture of 3   Percent cocoa of a mixture of 2
   parts Silky Dark Chocolate and 1 part   parts Rich Milk Chocolate and 1 part
   Smooth White Chocolate   Silky Dark Chocolate

6.   The average of 6 numbers is 44
                           The average of two of those numbers is 11

Quantity A   **Quantity B**

The average of the other 4 numbers   77

7.   Tavi drives 113 miles at 50 miles per hour and returns
                           via the same route at 60 miles per hour

Quantity A   **Quantity B**

Tavi's average speed for the entire round trip   55 mph

8.   Joe reaches into a bag containing 5 red, 4 blue, and 8 orange jellybeans
                        and randomly selects three jellybeans

Quantity A   **Quantity B**

The probability of selecting a red,   The probability of selecting a red, then
then a blue, then an orange jellybean   another red, then an orange jellybean

9.   Preeti can make 100 sandwiches in 1 hour and 15 minutes
                       Mariska can make 50 sandwiches in 30 minutes

Quantity A   **Quantity B**

The time it would take Preeti and   The time it would take to make 110
Mariska to make a total of 180   sandwiches if Mariska worked alone for
sandwiches, each working at her   thirty minutes and then Mariska and
own independent rate   Preeti worked together to finish the job

10.   A particular train travels from Town A to Town B at x miles per hour
                    and then from Town B to Town C at $1.2x$ miles per hour

Quantity A   **Quantity B**

The train's travel time from   The train's travel time from
Town A to Town B   Town B to Town C

Answer Key

1. D   2. C   3. A   4. C   5. C   6. B   7. B   8. C   9. A   10. D

Solutions

1. **D:** While we have the red-to-black ratios for each of the two bags, we don't have any real numbers of marbles anywhere, so it's impossible to combine the two ratios. Here we can try to prove D. For instance, let's say each bag contains 7 marbles. In such a case, Bag A would have 3 red and 4 black, and Bag B would have 3 black and 4 red. Quantity A and Quantity B would then each be equal to 7.

However, what if Bag A contains 7 marbles and Bag B contains 700 marbles? Then Bag A would have 3 red and 4 black, and Bag B would have 400 red and 300 black. In such a case, Quantity A would be equal to 403 and Quantity B would be equal to 304.

The answer is D.

2. **C:** First, let's see whether there's a shortcut here. June can run 6 laps in x minutes. If Miriam were equally fast, she could run 12 laps in $2x$ minutes (twice the laps in twice the time). As it turns out, Miriam can only do 11 laps in that time, so Miriam is slightly slower than June. If the columns then asked us for June and Miriam's times to run *the same number of laps,* we would not have to do any calculating: June is faster, so Miriam's time would be greater. However, we are asking June (the slightly faster person) to run slightly more laps, so it's pretty hard to estimate. Instead, we will use Rate × Time = Distance.

Since Rate × Time = Distance, Rate is equal to $\dfrac{\text{Distance}}{\text{Time}}$. Thus:

June's rate is $\dfrac{6}{x}$

Miriam's rate is $\dfrac{11}{2x}$

Quantity A asks for June's time to run 24 laps. Since Rate × Time = Distance, Time is equal to $\dfrac{\text{Distance}}{\text{Rate}}$. Therefore:

$$T = \dfrac{24}{\dfrac{6}{x}}$$
$$T = 24 \times \dfrac{x}{6}$$
$$T = 4x$$

June's time is $4x$.

Quantity B asks for Miriam's time to run 22 laps. Given that Time is equal to Distance/Rate:

$$T = \frac{22}{\frac{11}{2x}}$$

$$T = 22 \times \frac{2x}{11}$$

$$T = 4x$$

Miriam's time is also $4x$.

The answer is C.

3. **A:** This is an excellent example of a Word Problems problem for which no real calculation is needed if the idea of weighted averages is understood. Abe's current average is 68 (for a quick average, note that two scores ARE 68, and of the other two scores, one is six points over 68 and one is six points under 68, keeping the overall average at 68). Ben's average is also 68 (halfway between 66 and 70).

For Abe to get a 70 overall, his fifth score will have to compensate for 4 too-low scores. For Ben to get a 70 overall, his third score will only have to compensate for 2 too-low scores. So Abe will need a higher score to raise his average to 70 than Ben will. (All of us know from experience that the more bad grades you have, the higher you have to get on the next quiz to pull your average back up!)

Actually doing this problem mathematically would take too much time, but for the curious, Abe's fifth score could be calculated as such:

$$\frac{62 + 68 + 74 + 68 + x}{5} = 70$$

As it turns out, Abe needs a 78.

Ben's third score could be calculated as such:

$$\frac{66 + 70 + x}{3} = 70$$

Ben needs a 74.

The answer is A.

4. **C:** There's no shortcut to find the average here. Simply add $2 + 3 + 5 + 2 + 11 + 1$ to get 24 and divide by 6 to get 4. Quantity A is therefore equal to 4.

Finding the mode is much easier (the mode is simply the number that occurs most often in the list). The current mode is 2. When you double everything in the list, the mode will then be 4. (The other numbers in the list are irrelevant—don't bother to double them).

The answer is C.

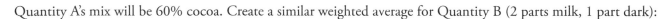

5. **C:** In Quantity A, we need the percent cocoa of a mix that is 3 parts dark and one part smooth white. So, you will need to create a weighted average (that is, you need to count the dark chocolate three times in the average, since there's three times as much of it):

$$\frac{80+80+80+0}{4} = 60$$

Quantity A's mix will be 60% cocoa. Create a similar weighted average for Quantity B (2 parts milk, 1 part dark):

$$\frac{50+50+80}{3} = 60$$

Quantity B's mix will also be 60% cocoa.

The answer is C.

6. **B:** No actual calculation is required here. 6 numbers average to 44 and two of them average to 11. That is, two of the numbers have an average that is 33 points below the overall average. Therefore, the other 4 numbers must bring the average up 33 points. However, since there are FOUR numbers bringing the average up (versus TWO bringing the average down), each of the individual numbers doesn't have to "compensate" as much—they will not have to be as high as 77, which is 33 points above 44.

Put another way, since there are only two numbers dragging the average down, they have to be pretty extreme. But since there are four numbers dragging the average up, they get to share the burden—they don't have to be as extreme.

The answer is B.

If you can master that logic, you can solve problems like this one very fast. However, if you prefer a more mathematical approach:

> If 6 numbers average to 44, their sum is $6 \times 44 = 264$.
> If 2 of the numbers average to 11, their sum is $2 \times 11 = 22$.
> Thus, the other 4 numbers must sum to $264 - 22 = 242$.
> $242 / 4 = 60.5$

Thus, the average of the other 4 numbers is 60.5, well under 77.

The answer is B.

7. **B:** No actual calculation is required here if you have a good grasp of average speed. First, Tavi's average speed is NOT 55 miles per hour—you cannot simply average the two speeds. Why? Because average speed is essentially what you would get if you clocked Tavi's speed during every second of the journey and then averaged all the seconds. If you wrote out a long, long list of all the numbers you'd be averaging, you'd have written out a lot more 50's than 60's, because Tavi spent more time driving at the slower speed. Therefore, Tavi's average speed will be "between 50 and 60 but closer to 50." (Note: this only works when the distances are *the same*). Therefore, 55 is higher than Tavi's average speed.

The answer is B.

8. C: Set up the probabilities in both columns before calculating either value. The bag contains 5 red, 4 blue, and 8 orange jellybeans, and thus 17 total jellybeans.

In Quantity A, the probability of picking a red is $\frac{5}{17}$. Keep in mind that once the red is selected, there are only 16 jellybeans left in the bag, so the probability of then picking a blue is $\frac{4}{16}$, and then the probability of picking an orange is $\frac{8}{15}$. Thus, Quantity A is equal to $\frac{5}{17} \times \frac{4}{16} \times \frac{8}{15}$.

In Quantity B, the probability of picking a red first is, of course, still $\frac{5}{17}$. Notice that *once a red is picked first, there are now equal numbers of blues and reds left in the bag* (4 each). Thus, the probability of now picking another red is $\frac{4}{16}$ (equal to the probability in Quantity A of picking a blue at this point), and then the probability of picking an orange is still $\frac{8}{15}$. Thus, Quantity B is also equal to $\frac{5}{17} \times \frac{4}{16} \times \frac{8}{15}$.

The answer is C.

You may have been tempted to multiply the fractions, but in this case no computation is necessary.

9. A: To get started on a work problem, we need to convert Preeti and Mariska's sandwich speeds into rate format—that is, we need their information in a "per hour" format. If Preeti can make 100 sandwiches in 1 hr 15 min, that's 100 sandwiches in 75 minutes:

$$\frac{100 \text{ sandwiches}}{75 \text{ minutes}} = \frac{x \text{ sandwiches}}{60 \text{ minutes}}$$

$$6{,}000 = 75x$$
$$x = 80$$

Therefore, Preeti can make 80 sandwiches per hour.

Mariska's rate is much easier—if she can make 50 sandwiches in 30 minutes, just double the rate to get that she can make 100 sandwiches in one hour.

Now that the rates are in "per hour" format, we can add. 80 sandwiches/hour + 100 sandwiches/hour is a combined rate of 180 sandwiches/hour.

Fortunately, Quantity A asks for their time to make 180 sandwiches working together, so Quantity A is simply equal to 1 hour.

Quantity B asks for the time it would take to make 110 sandwiches if Mariska worked alone for thirty minutes and then the women finished the job together. Working alone for 30 minutes, Mariska will make 50 sandwiches. That leaves 60 sandwiches left for the two of them to make together:

$$\frac{180 \text{ sandwiches}}{60 \text{ minutes}} = \frac{60 \text{ sandwiches}}{x \text{ minutes}}$$

$$180x = 3600$$
$$x = 20$$

Or, try this mental math shortcut: since the women working together can make 180 sandwiches/hour, it will take $\frac{1}{3}$ of the time to make $\frac{1}{3}$ of the sandwiches, so it will take $\frac{1}{3}$ of an hour, or 20 minutes.

Either way, Quantity B is equal to the 30 minutes Mariska works alone, plus the 20 minutes it takes the women to finish the job together. Thus, Quantity B is equal to 50 minutes.

The answer is A.

10. **D:** As a reminder: whenever you see a word problem on Quantitative Comparisons, *make sure you have the information you need before doing any computation.*

Quantities A and B ask about travel time. From Rate × Time = Distance, we need both distance and rate in order to compute time. The Common Information gives us only two relative rates (x and $1.2x$). Without some information about the distances from A to B and B to C, there is no way to compute even a relative time.

The answer is D.

Chapter 8
of

QUANTITATIVE COMPARISONS &
DATA INTERPRETATION

DATA

INTERPRETATION

In This Chapter . . .

- The Basic Process of Solving a Data Interpretation Question

- Data Interpretation Graphs and Charts

- Other Common Types of Diagrams

- Questions That Typically Require Input From More Than One Graph To Solve

DATA INTERPRETATION QUESTIONS

Overview

Data Interpretation questions appear as sets of problems that refer to the same group of one to three related graphs or charts. On the revised GRE, you will see an average of two Data Interpretation sets per exam, each with two or three associated problems.

Data Interpretation questions are not, in general, particularly difficult. However, they can take a lot of time to solve if you aren't careful. It is very important to learn how to tackle them efficiently, using the on-screen calculator when appropriate.

The Basic Process of Solving a Data Interpretation Question

1. Scan the graph(s). (15–20 sec)

- What type of graph is it?
- Is the data displayed in percentages or absolute quantities?
- Does the graph provide any overall total value?

2. Figure out what the question is asking. What does it ask you to do?

- Calculate a value?
- Establish how many data points meet a criterion?

3. Find the graph(s) with the needed information.

- Look for keywords in the question.

4. IF you need to establish how many data points meet a criterion, keep track as you go by taking notes.

5. IF you need to perform a computation, translate the question into a mathematical expression BEFORE you try to solve it.

6. IF one of the answer choices is "cannot be determined," check that you have ALL the information you need before performing any calculations.

7. Use the calculator when needed, but keep your eye out for opportunities to use time-saving estimation techniques.

- Does the question use the word approximate?
- Are the numbers in the answer choices sufficiently far apart?

Note that you will not always have to do all of the steps. This list of steps should be used as a high-level process checklist, to help you remember what to look for and do as you solve. The examples on the subsequent pages follow this process and show how to apply it to various types of problems.

Data Interpretation Graphs and Charts—aka—The Graph Zoo

Most GRE DI questions focus on data in five standard formats. You will be much faster at extracting the data if you are already familiar with reading these types of tables and graphs. GRE DI charts always tell a data story, and the questions you will be answering are about that story. In order to understand these charts and how they work, we will be looking at a simple data story about a produce stand. The owner of the produce stand has some numbers for the amounts of the different types of produce sold per month over a one-year period. For one month, the owner also has some detailed data on exactly which fruits and vegetables were sold. How might the GRE present this story? There are various ways, but all involve the five basic types of charts.

As you work through the examples, you will notice that many problems also involve FDP calculations, and you will find that you will be much faster at those calculations if you already know various standard formulas, such as the percentage increase/decrease formula, and computation shortcuts, such as estimating fractions. You will also notice that the solutions to the problems point out the various computation tricks. Use the calculator when it's easy to, but also work on developing estimation techniques. This will ultimately save you time.

Look carefully at the solutions and you will also see that they follow our previously described problem solving process. As an exercise, you might want to cover up the solution steps with a piece of paper and see if you can predict, from the general problem solving process, what the next step should be as you work through the solution and uncover each step. Although there are many ways to solve these problems, time is critical on the GRE and learning to follow a standard process and use computation shortcuts will ultimately save you a great deal of time and stress.

Pie Charts

A pie chart is used to show the relative sizes of "slices" as proportions of a whole. The size of the angle of the pie slice is proportional to the percentage of the whole for each item. Even if a pie chart shows amounts instead of percentages, data is shown in pies because percentages, or relative quantities, are important to the story. If you see data in a pie chart on the GRE, you know that there will be one or more questions about percentages or proportions.

Also, many pie charts include a a total amount annotated on the chart. If you see this feature , you can be almost certain that the GRE will ask you to calculate an absolute quantity of some item shown in the pie and that the best way to do so will be to use that number and multiply it by the relevant percentage. One pie can only show one series of data.

A pie chart can only show one series of data, so if you see two pies, which sometimes occurs on the GRE, they represent two series of data and you can be just about certain that one or more of the questions will ask you to compare something in the two different data series.

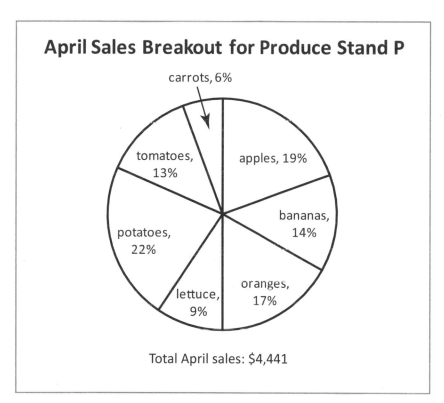

Some common calculations that you might be asked to perform on the example pie chart above, which shows the April sales breakout for our produce stand, are:

- Tomato sales = 13% of $4,441 = 0.13 × 4,441
- Lettuce & tomato sales = 9% of $4,441 + 13% of $4,441 = 22% of $4,441 = 0.22 × 4,441

1. Approximately what amount of total sales in April came from sales of apples, bananas, and oranges?

    (A) $2,221   (B) $2,362   (C) $2,495   (D) $2,571   (E) $2,683

- The question asks for the sum of the absolute dollar amount of total sales of apples, bananas, and oranges.

- The only chart we have is a pie chart showing percentages, so this question is asking us to convert from percents to dollar amounts.

- We have apples at 19%, bananas at 14%, and oranges at 17%, and total sales were $4,441.

- So we need to set up a mathematical expression for the amount of sales that come from apples, bananas, and oranges.

 $(0.19 \times 4,441) + (0.14 \times 4,441) + (0.17 \times 4,441) = 2,220.5$

You can also do this without a calculator:

$= 4,441 \times (0.19 + 0.14 + 0.17)$	factor the 4,441 to make the computation easier!
$= 4,441 \times (0.50)$	sum the percentage so we only multiple by one number
$= 4,441 \div 2$	50% of something is just half of it, and dividing by 2 is easy
$= 2,220.5$	the question says approximate, so A must be the answer

 2. If sales of potatoes were to increase by $173 next month and sales of all other items were held constant, approximately what percentage of the total sales would be potatoes?

    (A) 20%   (B) 25%   (C) 30%   (D) 35%   (E) 40%

- The question asks the new ratio of potato sales to total sales, after we add $173 in potato sales.

- The only chart we have is a pie chart showing percentages, but it has a total quantity and a percentage from potatoes

- We have 22% of total sales from potato sales and $4,441 in total sales.

- Set up a mathematical expression.

- $\dfrac{0.22(4,441)+173}{4,441+173} = 0.249 \approx 25\%$

- The answer is B.

3. If the areas of the sectors in the circle graph are drawn in proportion to the percentages shown, what is the approximate measure, in degrees, of the sector representing the percent of total sales due to lettuce?

   (A) 24 degrees   (B) 28 degrees   (C) 32 degrees   (D) 36 degrees   (E) 40 degrees

- The question asks for the degree measure of the lettuce wedge on the chart.

- The only chart we have is a pie chart showing percentages; that's the chart we use.

- We have 9% of total sales from lettuce, so lettuce represents 9% of the 360-degree circle.

- Writing this in math form, we get:

  $0.09 \times 360 = 32.4$ degrees

- The answer is C

Column Charts

A column chart shows amounts as heights. Often, the *x*-axis is time (e.g., months, years) and column charts are used to show trends over time.

Often the hardest thing about a column chart is just reading the values. The GRE never makes an exact value reading critical to answering a question unless numeric values are explicitly given (and even then you can usually just round), so just raise your index finger up near the computer monitor, draw an imaginary line across the chart, and estimate approximate quantities.

Single Series Column Charts

A single data series chart is so straightforward that it doesn't usually even have a legend. Here is an example showing the produce stand's sales:

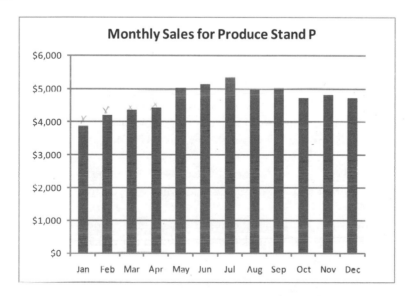

Some common calculations that you might be asked to perform are percentage increase or decrease from one time period to the next, or even more simply, just counting the number of periods when data values were above or below a particular value:

- Approximate percentage increase in sales from April to May

$$\frac{\text{May sales} - \text{April sales}}{\text{April sales}} \approx \frac{5,000 - 4,500}{4,500} = \frac{500}{4,500} \approx 11\%$$

- Number of months when sales were less than February sales = 1

---

1. In how many of the months shown were total produce sales greater than $4,600?

    (A) 7   (B) 8   (C) 9   (D) 10   (E) 11

- The question asks us to count the number of months shown that were greater than $4,600.

- The only chart we have is this column chart, and it shows the sales for each month directly, so we can just read the chart.

Counting Shortcut

- Since most months appear to have sales greater than $4,600, count the number of months in which sales were less than $4,600 and subtract.

- Months when sales were less than $4,600: Jan, Feb, Mar, Apr, so number of months when sales > $4,600 = 12 − 4 = 8, and the answer is B.

Full Explanation

- If we didn't see the shortcut, we need to count May, Jun, Jul, Aug, Sep, Oct, Nov, Dec, so number of months when sales > $4,600 = 8, and the answer is B.

Problem Recap: Use a piece of paper or even your finger to make a straight edge from halfway between the $4,000 and the $5,000 to make reading the graph easier.

Stacked Column Charts

The GRE is especially fond of stacked column charts because they can be used to show two or more data series at a time, as differently shaded parts of one column. For instance, "Vegetable sales" and "Fruit sales" sum to "Total Sales." This makes it as easy to answer questions that ask about the total as it is with just a single data series in the chart.

However, it is a little harder to read off "Vegetable Sales" by itself—you have to subtract "Total Sales" minus "Fruit Sales," so you can be almost certain that you will have a question that asks you to do something like this.

Notice also in the example below, which breaks out the monthly sales of the produce stand into fruit and vegetable sales, that charts that show multiple data series have legends so you can tell which part of the bar represents which category.

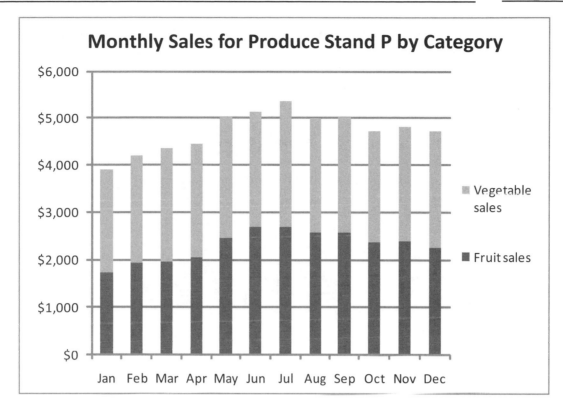

2. Approximately what were total vegetable sales in September?

(A) $5,000   (B) $4,000   (C) $3,000   (D) $2,500   (E) $2,000

- The question asks us to figure out vegetable sales in September.

- The only chart we have is this column chart, and it shows the vegetable sales for each month directly, so we can just read the chart.

- To get vegetable sales, we need total sales minus fruit sales. For September, that is equal to about $5,000 − $2,500 = $2,500 and the answer is D.

Problem Recap: Subtract in order to calculate values shown in stacked bar graphs.

Clustered Column Charts

Another variation on column charts has clustered columns instead of stacked columns. Clustered column charts make it easier to compare the parts of the total, but more difficult to determine the actual total because you have to sum the columns.

The types of questions that would be asked about a clustered column chart are the same as those that would be asked about a stacked column chart. The only difference between the two types is that it is easier to read a total quantity off of a stacked column chart, but easier to read the height of an individual series item, such as total vegetable sales in June, off of a clustered column chart. The example below shows exactly the same data as the stacked column chart above showed, except in the clustered column format.

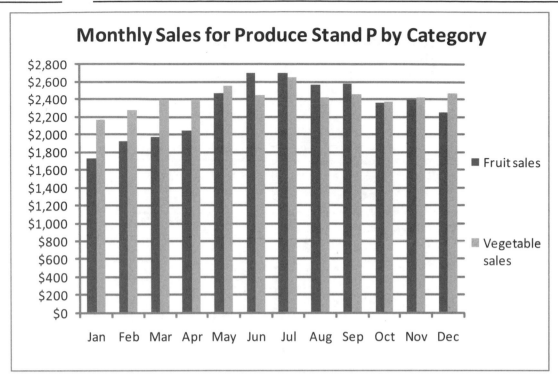

3. Which month had the largest percentage of vegetable sales relative to total sales?

(A) Jan   (B) Mar   (C) Jun   (D) Oct   (E) Nov

- The question asks us to compare the ratio of vegetable sales to total sales for several months.

- The only chart we have is this column chart, and it shows the sales for each month directly, so we can just read the numbers and calculate the ratios.

- The formula for the ratio of vegetable sales to total sales is just:

$$\frac{\text{vegetable sales}}{\text{fruit sales} + \text{vegetable sales}}$$

- The key to solving this problem is realizing that we don't have to do calculations for all of the months. In January and March, vegetable sales were substantially larger than fruit sales, so they were more than half of total sales, whereas in June, October, and November, they were about the same or actually less than fruit sales, so the only months we really have to look at are January and March.

Estimation Shortcut

- Since the difference in fruit and vegetable sales is about the same in both months, but total sales are much greater in March, the same absolute difference in fruit sales is a bigger percentage of the total sales in January than it is in March, so the answer is A.

<u>Full Explanation</u>

$$\frac{\text{Jan. vegetable sales}}{\text{Jan. vegetable sales} + \text{Jan. fruit sales}} \approx \frac{2,200}{1,700 + 2,200} = \frac{2,200}{3,900} \approx 0.56$$

$$\frac{\text{Mar. vegetable sales}}{\text{Mar. vegetable sales} + \text{Mar. fruit sales}} \approx \frac{2,400}{2,000 + 2,400} = \frac{2,200}{4,400} \approx 0.55$$

- So, of the months that are possible answers, January has the largest percentage of vegetable sales relative to total sales and the answer is A.

Problem Recap: Any given amount is a larger percentage of a smaller number than it is of a bigger number.

Percentage Column Charts

Occasionally the GRE uses column charts to show percentages directly, rather than absolute quantities. If you see this type of chart, and you need quantity information, you will need another chart to provide actual values.

Otherwise, the types of questions that would be asked about a percentage column chart are the same as those that would be asked about a stacked column chart. The example below shows a typical percentage column chart.

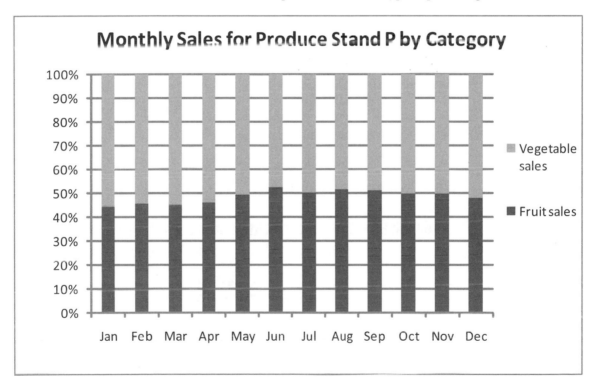

> 4. If the total produce sales in July at Produce Stand P were $4,500, what were the approximate total fruit sales in December at Produce Stand P?
>
>   (A) $2,100   (B) $2,200   (C) $2,300   (D) $2,400   (E) Cannot be determined

- The question asks us to determine the amount of fruit sales in December.

- The only chart we have is this column chart, and it shows the percentage of sales due to fruit and the percentage of sales due to vegetables for each month.

- The formula for the amount of fruit sales in December is just:

  total fruit sales in December = % fruit sales × total sales in December

- However, we have no information on total sales in December! We cannot assume that total sales in December are the same as in July, so we cannot answer this question. The answer is E.

Problem Recap: Be careful of the difference between charts that show percentages and charts that show actual quantities.

Line Charts

Line charts are very similar to column charts, but each amount is shown as a floating dot instead of as a column, and the dots are connected by lines. As is true with column charts, often, the *x*-axis is time (e.g., months, years) and line charts are used to show trends over time. Because of the continuous nature of lines, data series that are shown in line charts are almost always continuous values for something, and not separate categories, as they sometimes are in column charts.

Here is an example showing the produce stand's sales in a line chart:

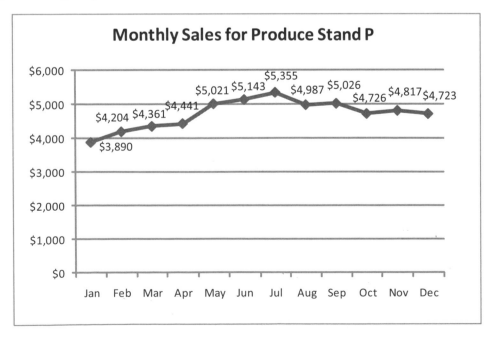

Some common calculations that you might be asked to perform are percentage increase or decrease from one time period to the next, the change in the overall average value of the data points if one of them changes, or even more simply, a count of the number of periods when data values were above or below a particular level:

- Approximate percentage increase in sales from April to May

$$\frac{\text{May sales} - \text{April sales}}{\text{April sales}} \approx \frac{5,021 - 4,441}{4,441} \approx 11\%$$

- Number of months when sales were less than July sales = 11

✓1. If the average sales per month at Produce Stand P were calculated at $4,725, and then it was discovered that the sales in January were actually $4,072 instead of the amount shown, what would the approximate correct average sales per month be?

    (A) $4,740   (B) $4,762   (C) $4,769   (D) $4,775   (E) Cannot be determined

---

- The average sales per month is just the total of all the monthly sales divided by the number of months.

- The only chart we have is this line chart, and it shows the monthly sales. The old amount for January was $3,890.

- The average formula is:

$$\text{old average} = 4,725 = \frac{\text{sum of 12 months of sales}}{12}$$

$$\text{new average} = \frac{\text{sum of 12 months of sales} - 3,890 + 4,072}{12}$$

Estimation Shortcut

- Since the total sum of the monthly sales has increased by 182, the average of the 12 monthly sales has increased by about $182/12 \approx 15$, so the answer is A.

Full Explanation

$$\text{new average} = \frac{\text{sum of 12 months of sales} - 3,890 + 4,072}{12}$$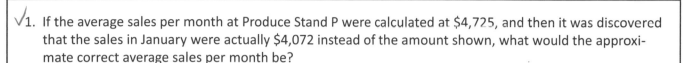

$$= \frac{\text{sum of 12 months of sales} + 182}{12}$$

$$= \frac{\text{sum of 12 months of sales}}{12} + \frac{182}{12}$$

$$\approx 4,725 + 15$$

$$= 4,740$$

The correct answer is A.

Problem Recap: The GRE likes these changing average problems. Remember the average change estimation shortcut!

> ✓ 2. What was the approximate percent increase in total sales at Produce Stand P from January to June?
>
>   (A) 19%   (B) 24%   (C) 28%   (D) 32%   (E) 38%

- In order to calculate the percent increase from January to June, we need the total sales in January and the total sales in June.

- The only chart we have is this line chart, and it shows the monthly sales. The amount for January was $3,890 and the amount for June is $5,143.

- The percent increase formula is:

$$\frac{new - old}{old} = \frac{Jun\ sales - Jan\ sales}{Jan\ sales}$$

 $$\frac{Jun\ sales - Jan\ sales}{Jan\ sales} = \frac{5,143 - 3,890}{3,890} \approx 0.32$$

- The answer is D.

Problem Recap: Know the percent increase and decrease formulas!

Multi-line charts

The GRE is especially fond of multi-line charts because they can be used to show two or more data series at a time. Note that multi-line charts, like stacked and clustered column charts, have legends.

In the example below we have "Vegetable sales" and "Fruit sales." With line charts, you will have to sum data points to calculate a total, because a total line is seldom shown (column charts are used when the goal is to emphasize the total).

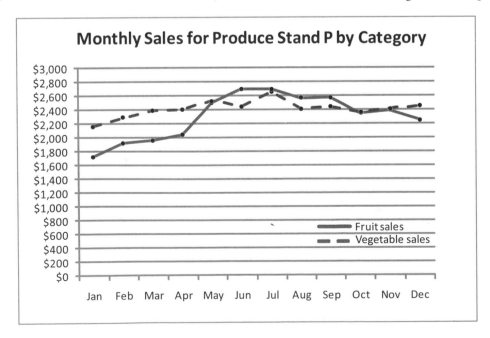

In addition to questions that require you to pick out data points from one of the data lines, expect that on at least a few questions that you will be asked to either combine or compare the data that make up one line to the data that make up the other.

- Approximate percentage increase in fruit sales from Jan to May

$$\frac{\text{May sales} - \text{Jan sales}}{\text{Jan sales}} \approx \frac{2{,}500 - 1{,}700}{1{,}700} \approx 47\%$$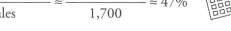

- Number of months when vegetable sales were more than \$100 greater than fruit sales = 6

✓ 3. In which of the following sequences of months did total sales decline the most?

　　(A) Feb–Mar　　　(B) Mar–Apr　　　(C) Jun–Jul　　　(D) Aug–Sep　　　(E) Sep–Oct

---

- Total sales are the sum of fruit and vegetable sales, and a decline means that at least one of the two would have to go down, and that drop would have to be bigger than any increase in the other category.

- The only chart we have is this line chart, and it shows the monthly sales, although it doesn't add them up for us.

- We hardly need a formula, because total sales are just fruit sales + vegetable sales.

Estimation Shortcut

- By scanning through the graph, we see that from Feb–Mar and Mar–Apr, both fruit and vegetable sales increased, so there was no decline. From Jun–Jul, vegetable sales increased, but fruit sales stayed flat, so still no decline. Aug–Sep also looks like a slight increase for both fruit and vegetable sales. However, from Sep–Oct, both fruit and vegetable sales seem to have declined, so the answer must be E.

Full Explanation

The long way to do this problem is to read both fruit and vegetable sales and calculate approximate total sales for each month. The answer is E.

Feb sales = 1,900 + 2,300 = 4,200 ⟩ Increase of 200
Mar sales = 2,000 + 2,400 = 4,400 ⟨ Increase of 200
Apr sales = 2,200 + 2,400 = 4,600 ⟩
Jun sales = 2,400 + 2,700 = 5,100 ⟩ Increase of 300
Jul sales = 2,700 + 2,700 = 5,400 ⟩
Aug sales = 2,400 + 2,600 = 5,000 ⟩ No change
Sep sales = 2,400 + 2,600 = 5,000 ⟨
Oct sales = 2,400 + 2,400 = 4,800 ⟩ At last! A monthly decrease

Problem Recap: Try visual estimation before performing calculations.

4. If the average price that the produce stand P sold fruit for in May was 80 cents per pound and the average wholesale cost to the produce stand in May of a pound of fruit was 25 cents per pound, approximately how much was produce stand P's gross profit on the sale of fruit in May?

(A) Cannot be determined   (B) $1,600   (C) $1,630   (D) $1,680   (E) $1,720

- To solve this, we need to remember that gross profit = sales revenue − costs. If we can plug in for fruit sales revenue and fruit cost, we can answer this question.

- The only chart we have is this line chart, and it shows the monthly fruit sales revenue in May, so we may be able to figure this out.

- The answer choices are too close together to estimate, so we'll have to calculate.

- We know that May fruit sales revenue ≈ $2,500. We know that the average wholesale cost per pound of fruit was $0.25 and that the average retail price per pound of fruit was $0.80.

- average gross profit per lb of fruit sold in May = 0.80 − 0.25 = 0.55

  gross profit on fruit sold in May = profit per lb × number of lbs of fruit sold
  = 0.55 × number of lbs of fruit sold

Calculation Technique

 $$\text{number of lbs of fruit sold in May} = \frac{\text{total fruit revenue}}{\text{revenue per lb}}$$

$$= \frac{2,500}{0.800} = 3,125$$

gross profit on fruit sold in May = profit per lb × number of lbs of fruit sold
= 0.55 × 3,125 = 1,718.75

- The answer is E.

Problem Recap: If you need a quantity, such as number of pounds of fruit sold, that is not directly shown in a graph, try writing out equations for it in terms of quantities you do know.

Bar Charts

A bar chart is essentially a column chart on its side. Although almost all bar charts on the GRE show absolute quantities, it is possible for them to show percentages. Because these more exotic charts are so rare on the GRE and are essentially types of column charts on their sides, we focus on standard bar charts in this section.

The GRE generally represents a single data series in each bar chart, and, like pie charts, some bar charts include a total amount annotated on the chart.

Here is an example showing the April sales breakout by item for produce stand P. The length of each bar represents either an absolute number or a percentage. In this case, it's an absolute number.

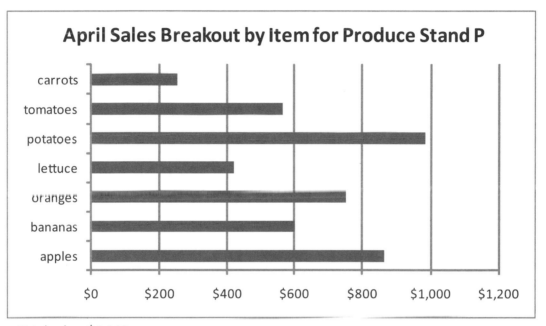

Total sales: $4,441

---

1. What fruit or vegetable generated the third highest sales in April for Produce Stand P?

   (A) tomatoes   (B) lettuce   (C) oranges   (D) bananas   (E) apples

---

- The question asks us to figure out the fruit or vegetable that generated the third highest sales in the month of April.

- The only chart we have is this bar chart, and it shows the sales for each fruit and vegetable in April.

- Scanning the chart, we see that potatoes had the highest sales, then apples, and third were oranges. So the answer must be C.

Problem Recap: Use a finger or a piece of paper to create a vertical line to help read bar chart values.

2. Which of the following ratios is closest to the ratio of carrot sales to potato sales at produce Stand P in the month of April

    (A) 1 : 4   (B) 2 : 9   (C) 1 : 5   (D) 1 : 6   (E) 3 : 10

- In order to calculate the ratio of carrot sales to potato sales in April, we need to know those amounts, and the chart gives them to us.

- The chart shows carrot sales were about $250 and potato sales were about $980.

 $$\frac{\text{carrot sales}}{\text{potato sales}} = \frac{250}{980} \approx 0.255 \approx \frac{1}{4}$$

- The answer is A.

Tables

A table is a very straightforward way to present data when calculations using that data are required because there is no need to estimate numbers. The thing that a table doesn't do, though, is allow you to easily see trends or estimate using visual techniques.

Often tables contain a mix of absolute quantities and percentage data. Be careful not to confuse the two. The GRE does not always label individual percents with a percentage sign. Rather, the entire row or column is generally labeled as such in the row or column header.

If you have to do calculations, and you probably will if you are given a table, it will be easy to look up the numbers. Here is an example of a table that combines absolute quantity information with percentage information for the produce stand.

Monthly Sales Breakout for Produce Stand P

Month	Total	% Fruit	% Vegetable
Jan	4121	44.29	55.71
Feb	4204	45.74	54.26
Mar	4361	45.10	54.90
Apr	4568	49.99	54.06
May	4791	49.17	50.83
Jun	4756	52.40	47.60
Jul	4822	50.38	49.62
Aug	4791	51.41	48.59
Sep	4801	51.21	48.79
Oct	4726	49.89	50.11
Nov	4817	49.78	50.22
Dec	4881	47.77	52.23

1. Approximately how many dollars worth of vegetables were sold in September, October, and November combined by produce stand P?

(A) $5,724   (B) $6,230   (C) $6,621   (D) $7,130   (E) $7,685

- The question asks us to calculate the dollars worth of vegetable sales in September, October, and November.

- We can do this because the chart shows the total sales for each month and the percentage of those sales that were due to vegetables. In September vegetables sales were 48.79% of $4,801, in October 50.11% of $4,726, and in November 50.22% of $4,817.

$$Sep + Oct + Nov \text{ vegetable sales} = 0.4879 \times 4{,}801 + 0.5011 \times 4{,}726 + 0.5022 \times 4{,}817$$

$$= 2{,}342.41 + 2{,}368.20 + 2{,}419.10 = 7{,}129.71$$

- The answer is D.

Other Common Types of Diagrams

Occasionally, other common types of diagrams, such as floor plans or outline maps, appear on the GRE. The good news is that although these diagrams are a little less familiar than the basic five, the questions that go with them tend to be a little bit easier. We've found questions that ask you to calculate surface area (of walls) and volume of rooms, but far fewer of the more challenging percent change and "how many points satisfy this complicated set of criteria" variety.

Questions That Typically Require Input From More Than One Graph To Solve

So far we've looked at the usual types of charts seen in GRE Data Interpretation and typical questions based on those charts. However, the GRE often complicates things by asking questions that require that we look up and integrate information from multiple charts. This type of "multi-graph" is not mathematically harder than a single graph question, but requires using data from two different graphs and so can be a bit more confusing. Efficient solving techniques and good scrap paper organization become even more valuable with multiple charts because more charts mean more opportunities to become confused and waste time. Our next example combines two types of charts that we've seen before and asks questions that require using information from both of them.

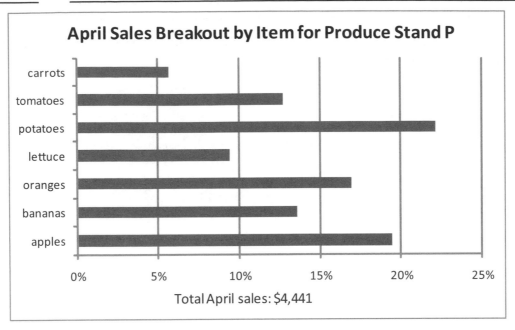

April Sales Breakout by Item for Produce Stand P

Total April sales: $4,441

Vitamin Content of Produce Items Sold at Produce Stand P in April

	Vitamin C content	Vitamin A content
apples	low	low
bananas	medium	low ✓
oranges	high	medium ✓
lettuce	high	low ✓
potatoes	medium	low ✓
tomatoes	high	high ✓
carrots	low	high ✓

✓1. Approximately what were the total April sales of produce items at produce Stand P that were high in both vitamin A and vitamin C content?

(A) 451   (B) 488   (C) 577   (D) 624   (E) 683

- We need to figure out which produce items were high in both vitamin A and vitamin C and calculate the total sales of those items.

- The table shows us that only tomatoes are high in both vitamins A and C, so we need total tomato sales.

- The bar graph shows us that tomatoes account for about 13% of April sales and that total April sales were $4,441. So we need 13% of $4,441.

 $0.13 \times 4,441 = \$577.33$

- The answer is C.

*Manhattan*GRE*Prep

the new standard

2. Approximately what dollar amount of the produce sold by produce stand P in April had medium or high amounts of either vitamin A or vitamin C?

(A) Cannot be determined (B) $3,120 (C) $3,600 (D) $4,000 (E) $4,600

- We need to figure out which produce items were high or medium in either vitamin A or vitamin C and calculate the total sales of those items.

- The table shows us that bananas, oranges, lettuce, potatoes, tomatoes, and carrots are high in either vitamins A and C, so we need their total sales.

Calculation Shortcut

- Since most of the produce items are high or medium in either vitamin A or vitamin C, it will be faster to just calculate the dollar amount of the items sold that are low in both vitamin A and vitamin C and subtract that from the total dollar amount of sales. The table shows that the only produce item that meets these criteria are apples, and the bar graph shows that they accounted for ≈ 19% of total sales.

$0.19 \times 4,441 \approx 844$

$4,441 - 844 = 3,597$

- The answer is C.

Full Explanation

- The long way to do this problem is to sum up the percentages of each type of produce solve that has a medium or high level of vitamin A or C.

- To do this, we need to read a number of values off of the bar graph. Carrots are 6% of sales, tomatoes are ≈ 13%, potatoes are ≈ 22%, lettuce is ≈ 9%, oranges are ≈ 17%, and bananas are ≈ 14%.

$0.06 \times 4,441 = 0.13 \times 4,441 + 0.22 \times 4,441 + 0.17 \times 4,441 + 0.14 \times 4,441$
$= (0.06 + 0.13 + 0.22 + 0.09 + 0.17 + 0.14) \times 4,441$
$= 0.81 \times 4,441$
$= 3,597$

That was lots of work!

Problem Recap: Sometimes it is easier to calculate the percentage that does NOT satisfy a condition rather than calculate a percentage directly.

A Straightforward Data Interpretation Problem Set

Let's start with some practice on a straightforward data interpretation problem. Start by reading the question and the answers and formulating your plan of attack. You can follow along on scratch paper if you feel ready for practice problems, or just read through the steps and focus on learning the basic process.

Problem A:

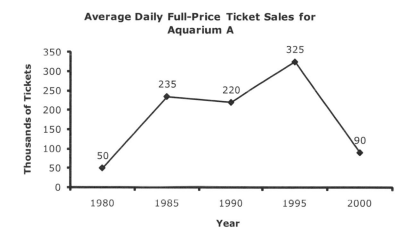

Average Daily Full-Price Ticket Sales for Aquarium A

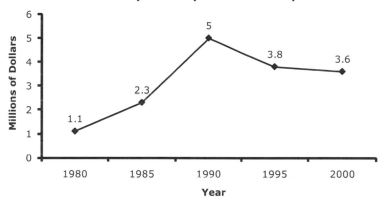

Total Yearly Gift-Shop Revenue for Aquarium A

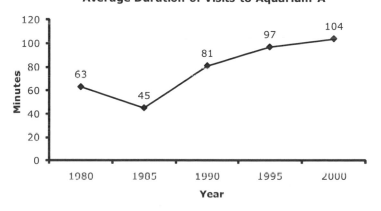

Average Duration of Visits to Aquarium A

The preceding three graphs are the data for the five questions that will follow. Since you've read this chapter, you know that it is a good idea to scan the graphs before looking at the problems to get a general sense of what information the graphs contain.

---

1. In how many years shown was the average duration of visits to Aquarium A more than twice as much as the average in 1985?

   (A) Four   (B) Three   (C) Two   (D) One   (E) None

---

2. In 1980, if a full-price ticket cost $4.70, what would have been the average daily revenue, in thousands of dollars from the sale of full-price tickets?

---

3. In 2000, the total number of dollars of gift-shop revenue was how many times as great as the average daily number of full-price tickets sold?

   (A) 400   (B) 200   (C) 80   (D) 40   (E) 20

---

4. What was the approximate percent increase in average daily full-price ticket sales from 1990 to 1995?

   (A) 10%   (B) 20%   (C) 33%   (D) 48%   (E) 66%

---

5. Which of the following statements can be inferred from the data?

   ☐ In each of the 5-year periods shown in which yearly gift-shop revenue decreased, average daily full-price ticket sales also decreased.

   ☐ The greatest increase in total yearly gift-shop revenue over any 5-year period shown was 2.7 million.

   ☐ From 1995 to 2000 the average duration of visits to the museum increased by 12 minutes.

An Example Mixing Percents and Absolute Quantities

It is very common in GRE data interpretation problems to see a set of graphs that incorporate both percentage and absolute quantity data. Being able to quickly and confidently combine these two types of data is a critical success factor for many medium to hard data interpretation problems. The following problems are typical examples.

Problem B:

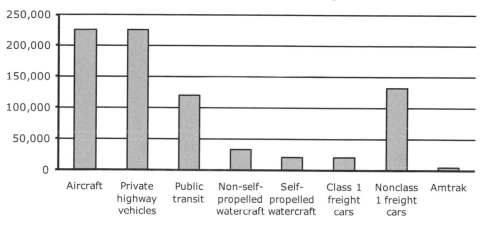

U.S. Aircraft, Vehicles, and Other Conveyances: 2000

total conveyances: 785,000

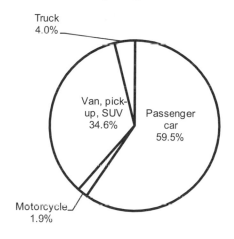

Private Highway Vehicles: 2000

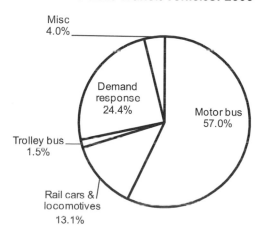

Public Transit Vehicles: 2000

If you scanned the graphs before looking at the problems, you know that the graphs have to do with absolute numbers of vehicles (the bar graph) and some additional information on the percentages of specific types of public transit and private highway vehicles in 2000. Also notice that the bar graph has a total conveyances line at the bottom, which may prove useful.

---

1. Approximately what was the ratio of trucks to passenger cars?

   (A) 1 to 20   (B) 1 to 18   (C) 1 to 17   (D) 1 to 15   (E) 1 to 12

---

2. Approximately how many more miscellaneous public transit vehicles than public transit trolley buses were there in 2000?

   (A) 1,000   (B) 1,500   (C) 2,000   (D) 2,500   (E) 3,000

---

3. If the number of aircraft, vehicles, and other conveyances was 572,000 in 1995, what was the approximate percentage increase from 1995 to 2000?

   (A) 37%   (B) 32%   (C) 27%   (D) 20%   (E) 15%

---

4. In 2000, if an equal percentage of passenger cars and demand-response vehicles experienced mechanical problems, and the number of passenger cars that experienced such problems was 13,436, approximately how many demand-response vehicles experienced mechanical problems?

   (A) 1,352   (B) 2,928   (C) 4,099   (D) 7,263   (E) 9,221

A Very Challenging Example, Requiring Excellent Technique

The following set is tricky. The graphs are a bit more complicated than is typical on the GRE. (Note that, because the GRE is a computer-adaptive test, only those already performing at a high level on the Quant section would ever see a Data Interpretation set this difficult.)

Problem C:

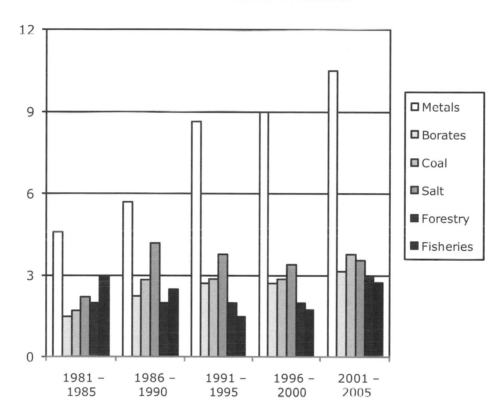

Natural Resource Industries' Output as a Percentage of Gross Domestic Product in Province P

Mining Industries' Average Annual Production

| Years | Mining Industries' Average Annual Production, in millions of 2005 dollars | Percentage of Mining Industries' Production | | | | | |
| | | Metals | | | Other Mined Products | | |
		Uranium, Titanium, & Aluminum	Gold & Silver	Copper	Borates	Coal	Salt
1981–1985	$342.5	10	20	16	15	17	22
1986–1990	$326.8	12	17	9	15	19	28
1991–1995	$310.0	16	20	12	15	16	21
1996–2000	$257.9	12	22	16	15	16	19
2001–2005	$205.0	14	24	12	15	18	17

1. Approximately what percent of the mining industries' average annual production in 1991–1995 came from production of aluminum?

   (A) 4%   (B) 7%   (C) 11%   (D) 22%   (E) It cannot be determined from the information given.

2. Approximately what percent of average annual GDP of Province P from 1996-2000 came from copper production?

   (A) 3%   (B) 6%   (C) 9%   (D 14%   (E) 18%

3. Which of the following statements can be inferred from the information given?

   ☐ For all the time periods shown, borate production, in millions of 2005 dollars, was the same.

   ☐ Of the time periods shown, 1981–1985 was the one in which the mining industries produced the greatest value of gold and silver, measured in 2005 dollars.

   ☐ Of the time periods shown, 2001–2005 had the highest average annual GDP, measured in 2005 dollars.

Problem A Solutions:

1.

- To save time, write x for "the average duration of visits to the museum" when you rephrase the question:

  # of years x was $\geq 2 \times$ (avg. in 1985)

- The graph for x is the bottom one and the average in 1985 is 45

- Substitute this number into the above inequality:

  # of years x was $\geq 2 \times 45$
  $\qquad\qquad\qquad\geq 90$

- Count years with average ≥ 90. There are two (1995 and 2000).

- The answer is C.

Problem Recap: If there are no lines, use your finger to create a line on the screen to help you read approximate graph values.

2. Rephrase the question:

  1980 : av. daily ticket revenue = ?

- Average daily ticket revenue must equal (the price of one ticket) times (the number of tickets sold on an average day), so we can write:

  = ($4.70) $\times$ (av. daily ticket sales)

- The ticket sales graph is the top one and the average daily ticket sales for 1980 was 50 (in thousands).

- Substitute this number into the equation:

  = ($4.70)(50) = $235 (in thousands).

  Hit the "transfer" button on the calculator to transfer this number to the answer box.

Problem Recap: Note the perfect match up of the words. Both the graph and the question talk about "full-price ticket sales." If the question had talked about "ticket sale revenue instead," the answer would be "cannot be determined."

3.

- To save time, write x for "total number of dollars of gift-shop revenue" and y for "average daily number of full-price tickets" when you rephrase the question:

- In 2000, x how many times y?

- The relevant graph for x is the middle one and the value for x in 2000 is 3,600,000.

- The relevant graph for *y* is the top one and the value for *y* for 2000 is 90,000.

- Substitute these numbers into the question:

    3,600,000 how many times 90,000?

- Solve using division:

$$\frac{3,600,000}{90,000} = 40$$

    The answer is D.

Problem Recap: Write down data, equations, and math steps for multi-chart problems in order to reduce careless errors.

4. Note that the question asks you to approximate:

- To save time, write *x* for "average daily full price ticket sales" when you rephrase the question:

    % increase in *x* from 1990 to 1995 = ?

- By definition of "percent increase," this is

$$= \frac{(x \text{ in } 1995) - (x \text{ in } 1990)}{(x \text{ in } 1990)}$$

- The graph for *x* is the top one and *x* in 1990 is 220 and in 1995 is 325.

- Substitute these numbers into the equation:

$$= \frac{325 - 220}{220}$$
$$= \frac{105}{220} = 0.477 \approx 48\%$$

    The answer is D.

5.

- Since this question asks us which statements can be inferred from the data, we have to use the process of elimination and treat each statement as its own mini question.

- First statement: Identify the 5-year periods in which gift-shop revenue (middle graph) decreased: 1990–1995 & 1995–2000. Next, locate the graph for <u>average ticket sales</u>: TOP. Ticket sales did NOT decrease in 1990–1995, so statement I is FALSE.

- Second statement: The graph for <u>gift-shop revenue</u> is the middle one. Locate the biggest jump—it is from 2.3 to 5. Compute the size of this jump: 5 − 2.3 = 2.7, so statement II is TRUE.

- Third statement: The graph for <u>duration of visits</u> is the bottom one. The increase from 1995 to 2000 was $104 - 97 = 7$ minutes, not 12 minutes, so statement III is FALSE.

- Only the box for the second statement should be selected.

Problem Recap: Multi-statement problems are not necessarily hard, but they are confusing, so it is especially important to keep your scrap paper organized.

Problem B Solutions:

1.

- Rephrase the question as a mathematical expression. To save time, write x for "the number of trucks" and y for "the number of passenger cars" when you rephrase the question. Remember that a ratio is just a fraction, so

  "ratio of x to y" is just the English version of the mathematical expression $\dfrac{x}{y}$:

  What is $\dfrac{x}{y}$?

- We don't have direct data on either x or y, but the second pie graph tells us that trucks are 4.0% of private highway vehicles and passenger cars are 59.5% of private highway vehicles. Although the first graph tells us that the number of private highway vehicles is roughly 225,000, we don't need to use that information to get to the answer because the question just asks us about the ratio of x to y, and the percentages on the pie give us the ratio of x and y to the total number of private highway vehicles already, so multiplying both 0.04 and 0.595 by 225,000 would result in 225,000 being cancelled out of the fraction:

$$\frac{x}{y} = \frac{0.04 \times 225,000}{0.595 \times 225,000}$$

$$= \frac{0.04}{0.595} = \frac{4}{59.5} \quad \text{multiply both top and bottom by 100}$$

$$\approx \frac{4}{60} = \frac{1}{15}$$

- The answer is D

Problem Recap: In order to calculate a ratio directly, you need either both actual amounts OR both percentages.

2.

- Rephrase the question as a mathematical expression. To save time, write x for "the number of miscellaneous public transit vehicles" and y for "the number of public transit buses" when you rephrase the question:

  What is $x - y$?

- We don't have direct data on either x or y, but the first pie graph tells us that miscellaneous public transit vehicles are 4.0% of public transit vehicles and trolley buses are 1.5% of public transit vehicles. The first graph tells us that the number of public transit vehicles is roughly 120,000, so we can calculate $x - y$.

$$x - y = (0.04 \times 120,000) - (0.015 \times 120,000)$$
$$= (0.04 - 0.015) \times 120,000$$
$$= 0.025 \times 120,000$$
$$= 3,000$$

- The answer is E

Problem Recap: Notice that you can subtract the percents and then multiply by the total number of public transit vehicles to simplify the calculation.

3.

- Rephrase the question as a mathematical expression. To save time, write x for "the number of aircraft, vehicles, and other conveyances" when you rephrase the question. The key thing to remember here is the percent increase formula:

$$\frac{New - Old}{Old}$$

So the percent increase in x from 1995 to 2000 $= \dfrac{x \text{ in } 2000 - x \text{ in } 1995}{x \text{ in } 1995}$

- The question says that x in 1995 was 572,000. At first, it might appear as if there is a need to sum the number of all of the different types of conveyances in the first chart in order to compute x in 2000, but notice that right underneath the title of the first chart is a line saying that the total number of conveyances is 785,000, so:

$$\frac{785,000 - 572,000}{572,000} \approx 0.372 \approx 37\%$$

- The answer is A.

Problem Recap: This problem takes much longer if you have to sum up the number of non-aircraft conveyances! Look for grand totals on graphs!

4.

- Rephrase the question as a mathematical expression. To save time, write x for "the number of demand-response vehicles that experience mechanical problems" when you rephrase the question. The key thing to remember here is the relationship between percentages and absolute numbers. Multiply the percentage times the total to get the absolute quantity.

If $\dfrac{13,436}{\text{total num passenger cars}} = \dfrac{x}{\text{total num dem-resp vehicles}}$, then what is x?

Rearrange to get: $x = \dfrac{13,436 \times (\text{total num dem-resp vehicles})}{\text{total num passenger cars}}$

- We know from the first pie that demand-response vehicles makes up 24.4% of all public transit vehicles, and we know from the main chart that there are roughly 120,000 public transit vehicles, so we can calculate the approximate number of demand-response vehicles:

$$0.244 \times 120,000 = 29,280$$

- We know from the second pie that passenger cars makes up 59.5% of all private highway vehicles, and we know from the main chart that there are about 225,000 private highway vehicles, so we can calculate the approximate number of private highway vehicles:

$$0.595 \times 225,000 = 133,875$$

- So, pulling it all together:

$$x = \frac{13,436 \times 29,280}{133,875} \approx 2,938$$

To avoid overloading the calculator display, you must divide 13,436 by 133,875 before multiplying by 29,280.

- The answer is B.

Problem C Solutions:

1.

- Since one of the answer choices is "cannot be determined" check exact wording and be sure you have enough information to solve it before doing any math.

- Locate the relevant column within the table in the chart on the bottom: "Uranium, Titanium, & Aluminum." The figures in this column represent Uranium + Titanium + Aluminum, but do not tell us the level of Aluminum *alone*. Since the question is asking *only* about Aluminum, we do not have enough information.

- The answer is E.

Problem Recap: This type of problem is very quick if you check to see whether you have enough information to answer the question before making any calculations.

2.

- Rephrase the question. Expressing the desired percentage as a fraction is a good way to abbreviate the question:

In 1996–2000, $\dfrac{\text{Copper}}{\text{GDP}} = ?$

- The chart that mentions Copper is on the bottom and tells us that in 1996–2000 Copper was 16% of Mining Industries' Production. In other words, it tells us that the value of $\frac{\text{Copper}}{\text{Mining}} = 0.16$. This is not quite what we are looking for, since the question is about $\frac{\text{Copper}}{\text{GDP}}$. Look to the top chart to see if it provides a way to convert our $\frac{\text{Copper}}{\text{Mining}}$ information into a $\frac{\text{Copper}}{\text{GDP}}$ figure.

- The top chart gives us information on Metals, Borates, Coal, and Salt—all of the components of Mining from the bottom table—as a percentage of GDP. We will therefore be able to use the following equation to get $\frac{\text{Copper}}{\text{GDP}}$:

$$\frac{\text{Copper}}{\text{GDP}} = \left(\frac{\text{Copper}}{\text{Mining}}\right) \times \left(\frac{\text{Mining}}{\text{GDP}}\right)$$

- Substitute numbers into the above equation. The top chart tells us that in 1996–2000 Metals were 9% of GDP and Borates, Coal, and Salt were each roughly 3% of GDP. Thus, total Mining was roughly 9% + 3% + 3% + 3% =18% of GDP in 1996–2000:

$$\frac{\text{Copper}}{\text{GDP}} = \left(\frac{\text{Copper}}{\text{Mining}}\right) \times \left(\frac{\text{Mining}}{\text{GDP}}\right)$$

$$\approx (16\%) \times (18\%) = (0.16) \times (0.18) = 0.029 \approx 3\%$$

- The answer is A.

Problem Recap: Write out equations with units to help yourself figure out what values you need.

3.

- First statement: For each time period, the production of Borates, in the bottom chart, is given as 15% of that period's Mining Industries' Production. Since each period has a *different* dollar figure for Mining Industries' Production, Borate production is not the same in all of the periods. (For example, in 1981–1985 Borate production was 15% × $342.5 whereas in 1986–1990 Borate production was 15% × $326.8 .) Statement I is therefore false.

- Second statement: To test whether this is true, notice that the dollar values of Gold & Silver production were:

81–85: 20% × $342.5
86–90: 17% × $326.8
91–95: 20% × $310
96–00: 22% × $257.9
01–05: 24% × $205

- We can eliminate two of these five choices without doing any arithmetic. The figure for 86–90 is clearly lower than that for 81–85, because 86–90 has a lower percentage (17% as opposed to 20%) times a lower dollar amount ($326.8 as opposed to $342.5). Along the same lines, we can see that 91–95 is lower than 81–85: the percentage is the same for both periods (20%), but for 91–95 that percentage is multiplied by a smaller dollar amount ($310 as opposed to $342.5). For the three remaining periods, use the calculator:

81–85: 20% × $342.5 = 68.50
96–00: 22% × $257.9 = 56.74
01–05: 24% × $205 = 49.20

- These calculations show that 81–85 had the highest Gold & Silver production, so statement II is true.

- Third statement: It concerns which period had the highest Gross Domestic Product (GDP). We clearly need to use the TOP chart, because it is the one that mentions GDP. However, the top chart is not enough, because it only gives information as *percentages*. To get dollar amounts for GDP, we need to connect the dollar amounts in the BOTTOM chart with the percentages in the top chart.

- One way to figure out GDP in 2001–2005 would be to focus on Salt. The top table gives us a figure for Salt as a percentage of GDP (roughly 3.5%), and the bottom table allows us to figure out the dollar amount of Salt production (17% × $205). Substituting these figures into the following equation, we could solve for GDP:

$$GDP = \frac{Salt}{\left(\dfrac{Salt}{GDP}\right)}$$

$$GDP = \frac{0.17 \times \$205}{3.596}$$

- However, performing this calculation, and similar calculations for other time periods, would be too much work. It is a good idea to focus on Borates instead, since Borates accounted for the *same* percentage (15%) of Mining Industries' Production in each of the time periods shown. Consider the equation:

$$GDP = \frac{Borates}{\left(\dfrac{Borates}{GDP}\right)}$$

- Compare 1981–1985 to 2001–2005. In 2001–2005 the numerator (Borates) of the fraction $\left(\dfrac{Borates}{\dfrac{Borates}{GDP}}\right)$ was *lower* than in any other time period—it was 15% of the *lowest* value ($205 million) for Mining Industries'

Production. On the other hand 2001–2005 saw the denominator $\left(\dfrac{Borates}{GDP}\right)$ of our large fraction assume its *highest* value ($\approx 3\%$), because the top chart shows that 2001–2005 was the only year in which

Borate production was more than 3% of GDP. Thus, $GDP = \dfrac{(0.015) \times (205 \text{ million})}{0.03}$ for 2001–2005.

In 1981–1985, Borates were 15% of a much larger total ($342.5 million) but were a smaller percentage of

GDP ($\approx 1.5\%$). So $GDP = \dfrac{(0.015) \times (342.5 \text{ million})}{0.015}$. This fraction has a larger numerator and a smaller denominator, which will result in a higher total GDP. Statement III is therefore false.

- Only the box for the second statement should be checked.

Problem Recap: On problems this difficult it is essential to AVOID HARD MATH even with a calculator, and rely on approximation and bounding instead. Using the calculator is helpful, but always look for quicker ways to arrive at a conclusion.

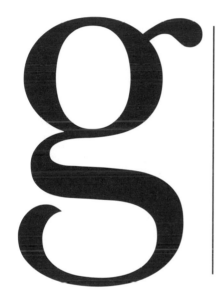

Appendix
of
QUANTITATIVE COMPARISONS & DATA INTERPRETATION

GRE GLOSSARY

Glossary

absolute value: The distance from zero on the number line for a particular term. E.g. the absolute value of −7 is 7 (written $|-7|$).

arc length: A section of a circle's circumference.

area: The space enclosed by a given closed shape on a plane; the formula depends on the specific shape. E.g. the area of a rectangle equals *length × width*.

axis: One of the two number lines (*x*-axis or *y*-axis) used to indicate position on a coordinate plane.

base: In the expression b^n, the variable *b* represents the base. This is the number that we multiply by itself *n* times. Also can refer to the horizontal side of a triangle.

center (circle): The point from which any point on a circle's radius is equidistant.

central angle: The angle created by any two radii.

circle: A set of points in a plane that are equidistant from a fixed center point.

circumference: The measure of the perimeter of a circle. The circumference of a circle can be found with this formula: $C = 2\pi r$, where *C* is the circumference and *r* is the radius.

coefficient: A number being multiplied by a variable. In the equation $y = 2x + 5$, the coefficient of the *x* term is 2.

common denominator: When adding or subtracting fractions, we first must find a common denominator, generally the smallest common multiple of both numbers.

Example:

> Given (3/5) + (1/2), the two denominators are 5 and 2. The smallest multiple that works for both numbers is 10. The common denominator, therefore, is 10.

composite number: Any number that has more than 2 factors.

constant: A number that doesn't change, in an equation or expression. We may not know its value, but it's "constant" in contrast to a variable, which varies. In the equation $y = 3x + 2$, 3 and 2 are constants. In the equation $y = mx + b$, *m* and *b* are constants (just unknown).

coordinate plane: Consists of a horizontal axis (typically labeled "*x*") and a vertical axis (typically labeled "*y*"), crossing at the number zero on both axes.

decimal: Numbers that fall in between integers. A decimal can express a part–to–whole relationship, just as a percent or fraction can.

Example:

> 1.2 is a decimal. The integers 1 and 2 are not decimals. An integer written as 1.0, however, is considered a decimal. The decimal 0.2 is equivalent to 20% or to 2/10 (= 1/5).

✓**denominator:** The bottom of a fraction. In the fraction (7/2), 2 is the denominator.

✓**diameter:** A line segment that passes through the center of a circle and whose endpoints lie on the circle.

✓**difference:** When one number is subtracted from another, the difference is what is left over. The difference of 7 and 5 is 2, because $7 - 5 = 2$.

✓**digit:** The ten numbers 0, 1, 2, 3, 4, 5, 6, 7, 8, and 9. Used in combination to represent other numbers (e.g., 12 or 0.38).

✓**distributed form:** Presenting an expression as a sum or difference. In distributed form, terms are added or subtracted. $x^2 - 1$ is in distributed form, as is $x^2 + 2x + 1$. In contrast, $(x + 1)(x - 1)$ is not in distributed form; it is in factored form.

✓**divisible:** If an integer x divided by another number y yields an integer, then x is said to be divisible by y.

Example:

> 12 divided by 3 yields the integer 4. Therefore, 12 is divisible by 3. 12 divided by 5 does not yield an integer. Therefore, 12 is not divisible by 5.

✓**divisor:** The part of a division operation that comes after the division sign. In the operation $22 \div 4$ (or 22/4), 4 is the divisor. Divisor is also a synonym for factor. See: factor

✓**equation:** A combination of mathematical expressions and symbols that contains an equals sign. $3 + 7 = 10$ is an equation, as is $x + y = 3$. An equation makes a statement: left side equals right side.

✓**equilateral triangle:** A triangle in which all three angles are equal; in addition, all three sides are of equal length.

✓**even:** An integer is even if it is divisible by 2. 14 is even because 14/2 = an integer (7).

✓**exponent:** In the expression b^n, the variable n represents the exponent. The exponent indicates how many times to multiple the base, b, by itself. For example, $4^3 = 4 \times 4 \times 4$, or 4 multiplied by itself three times.

✓**expression:** A combination of numbers and mathematical symbols that does not contain an equals sign. xy is an expression, as is $x + 3$. An expression represents a quantity. → *part of equation*

✓**factored form:** Presenting an expression as a product. In factored form, expressions are multiplied together. The expression $(x + 1)(x - 1)$ is in factored form: $(x + 1)$ and $(x - 1)$ are the factors. In contrast, $x^2 - 1$ is not in factored form; it is in distributed form.

✓**factor:** Positive integers that divide evenly into an integer. Factors are equal to or smaller than the integer in question. 12 is a factor of 12, as are 1, 2, 3, 4, and 6.

✓**factor foundation rule:** If a is a factor of b, and b is a factor of c, then a is also a factor of c. For example, 2 is a factor of 10. 10 is a factor of 60. Therefore, 2 is also a factor of 60.

factor tree: Use the "factor tree" to break any number down into its prime factors. For example: →

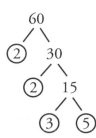

FOIL: First, Outside, Inside, Last; an acronym to remember the method for converting from factored to distributed form in a quadratic equation or expression. $(x + 2)(x - 3)$ is a quadratic expression in factored form. Multiply the First, Outside, Inside, and Last terms to get the distributed form. $x \times x = x^2$, $x \times -3 = -3x$, $x \times 2 = 2x$, and $2 \times -3 = -6$. The full distributed form is $x^2 - 3x + 2x - 6$. This can be simplified to $x^2 - x - 6$.

fraction: A way to express numbers that fall in between integers (though integers can also be expressed in fractional form). A fraction expresses a part-to-whole relationship in terms of a numerator (the part) and a denominator (the whole). (E.g. 3/4 is a fraction.)

hypotenuse: The longest side of a right triangle. The hypotenuse is opposite the right angle.

improper fraction: Fractions that are greater than 1. An improper can also be written as a mixed number. (7/2) is an improper fraction. This can also be written as a mixed number: 3½.

inequality: A comparison of quantities that have different values. There are four ways to express inequalities: less than (<), less than or equal to (≤), greater than (>), or greater than or equal to (≥). Can be manipulated in the same way as equations with one exception: when multiplying or dividing by a negative number, the inequality sign flips.

integers: Numbers, such as −1, 0, 1, 2, and 3, that have no fractional part. Integers include the counting numbers (1, 2, 3, ...), their negative counterparts (−1, −2, 3, ...), and 0.

interior angles: The angles that appear in the interior of a closed shape.

isosceles triangle: A triangle in which two of the three angles are equal; in addition, the sides opposite the two angles are equal in length.

line: A set of points that extend infinitely in one direction without curving. On the GRE, lines are by definition perfectly straight.

line segment: A continuous, finite section of a line. The sides of a triangle or of a rectangle are line segments.

linear equation: An equation that does not contain exponents or multiple variables multiplied together. $x + y = 3$ is a linear equation; $xy = 3$ and $y = x^2$ are not. When plotted on a coordinate plane, linear equations create lines.

mixed number: An integer combined with a proper fraction. A mixed number can also be written as an improper fraction. 3½ is a mixed number. This can also be written as an improper fraction: (7/2).

multiple: Multiples are integers formed by multiplying some integer by any other integer. 12 is a multiple of 12 (12 × 1), as are 24 (= 12 × 2), 36 (= 12 × 3), 48 (= 12 × 4), and 60 (= 12 × 5). (Negative multiples are possible in mathematics but are not typically tested on the GRE.)

negative: Any number to the left of zero on a number line; can be integer or non-integer.

negative exponent: Any exponent less than zero. To find a value for a term with a negative exponent, put the term containing the exponent in the denominator of a fraction and make the exponent positive. $4^{-2} = 1/4^2$. $1/3^{-2} = 1/(1/3)^2 = 3^2 = 9$.

$\mathcal{M}anhattan$GRE Prep
the new standard
163

number line: A picture of a straight line that represents all the numbers from negative infinity to infinity.

numerator: The top of a fraction. In the fraction, (7/2), 7 is the numerator.

odd: An integer that is not divisible by 2. 15 is odd because 15/2 is not an integer (7.5).

order of operations: The order in which mathematical operations must be carried out in order to simplify an expression. (See PEMDAS)

the origin: The coordinate pair (0,0) represents the origin of a coordinate plane.

parallelogram: A four-sided closed shape composed of straight lines in which the opposite sides are equal and the opposite angles are equal.

PEMDAS: An acronym that stands for Parentheses, Exponents, Multiplication, Division, Addition, Subtraction, used to remember the order of operations.

percent: Literally, "per one hundred"; expresses a special part-to-whole relationship between a number (the part) and one hundred (the whole). A special type of fraction or decimal that involves the number 100. (E.g. 50% = 50 out of 100.)

perimeter: In a polygon, the sum of the lengths of the sides.

perpendicular: Lines that intersect at a 90° angle.

plane: A flat, two-dimensional surface that extends infinitely in every direction.

point: An object that exists in a single location on the coordinate plane. Each point has a unique x-coordinate and y-coordinate that together describe its location. (E.g. (1, −2) is a point.)

polygon: A two-dimensional, closed shape made of line segments. For example, a triangle is a polygon, as is a rectangle. A circle is a closed shape, but it is not a polygon because it does not contain line segments.

positive: Any number to the right of zero on a number line; can be integer or non-integer.

prime factorization: A number expressed as a product of prime numbers. For example, the prime factorization of 60 is $2 \times 2 \times 3 \times 5$.

prime number: A positive integer with exactly two factors: 1 and itself. The number 1 does not qualify as prime because it has only one factor, not two. The number 2 is the smallest prime number; it is also the only even prime number. The numbers 2, 3, 5, 7, 11, 13 etc. are prime.

product: The end result when two numbers are multiplied together. (E.g. the product of 4 and 5 is 20.)

Pythagorean Theorem: A formula used to calculate the sides of a right triangle. $a^2 + b^2 = c^2$, where a and b are the lengths of the two legs of the triangle and c is the length of the hypotenuse of the triangle.

Pythagorean triplet: A set of 3 numbers that describe the lengths of the 3 sides of a right triangle in which all 3 sides have integer lengths. Common Pythagorean triplets are 3–4–5, 6–8–10 and 5–12–13.

quadrant: One quarter of the coordinate plane. Bounded on two sides by the x- and y-axes.

the new standard

quadratic expression: An expression including a variable raised to the second power (and no higher powers). Commonly of the form $ax^2 + bx + c$, where a, b, and c are constants.

quotient: The result of dividing one number by another. The quotient of $10 \div 5$ is 2.

radius: A line segment that connects the center of a circle with any point on that circle's circumference. Plural: radii.

reciprocal: The product of a number and its reciprocal is always 1. To get the reciprocal of an integer, put that integer on the denominator of a fraction with numerator 1. The reciprocal of 3 is (1/3). To get the reciprocal of a fraction, switch the numerator and the denominator. The reciprocal of (2/3) is (3/2).

rectangle: A four-sided closed shape in which all of the angles equal 90° and in which the opposite sides are equal. Rectangles are also parallelograms.

right triangle: A triangle that includes a 90°, or right, angle.

root: The opposite of an exponent (in a sense). The square root of 16 (written $\sqrt{16}$) is the number (or numbers) that, when multiplied by itself, will yield 16. In this case, both 4 and −4 would multiply to 16 mathematically. However, when the GRE provides the root sign for an even root, such as a square root, then the only accepted answer is the positive root, 4. That is, $\sqrt{16} = 4$, NOT +4 or −4. In contrast, the equation $x^2 = 16$ has TWO solutions, +4 and −4.

sector: A "wedge" of the circle, composed of two radii and the arc connecting those two radii.

simplify: Reduce numerators and denominators to the smallest form by taking out common factors. Dividing the numerator and denominator by the same number does not change the value of the fraction.

Example:

> Given (21/6), we can simplify by dividing both the numerator and the denominator by 3.
> The simplified fraction is (7/2).

slope: "Rise over run," or the distance the line runs vertically divided by the distance the line runs horizontally. The slope of any given line is constant over the length of that line.

square: A four-sided closed shape in which all of the angles are equal 90° and all of the sides are equal. Squares are also rectangles and parallelograms.

sum: The result when two numbers are added together. The sum of 4 and 7 is 11.

term: Parts within an expression or equation that are separated by either a plus sign or a minus sign. (E.g. in the expression $x + 3$, "x" and "3" are each separate terms).

triangle: A three-sided closed shape composed of straight lines; the interior angles add up to 180°.

two-dimensional: A shape containing a length and a width.

variable: Letter used as a substitute for an unknown value, or number. Common letters for variables are x, y, z and t. In contrast to a constant, we generally think of a variable as a value that can change (hence the term variable). In the equation $y = 3x + 2$, both y and x are variables.

x-axis: A horizontal number line that indicates left–right position on a coordinate plane.

x-coordinate: The number that indicates where a point lies along the *x*-axis. Always written first in parentheses. The *x*-coordinate of $(2, -1)$ is 2.

x-intercept: The point where a line crosses the *x*-axis (that is, when y = 0).

y-axis: A vertical number line that indicates up–down position on a coordinate plane.

y-coordinate: The number that indicates where a point lies along the *y*-axis. Always written second in parentheses. The y-coordinate of $(2, -1)$ is -1.

y-intercept: the point where a line crosses the *y*-axis (that is, when $x = 0$). In the equation of a line $y = mx + b$, the *y*-intercept equals b. Technically, the coordinates of the y-intercept are $(0, b)$.

mba Mission

Every candidate has a unique story to tell.

We have the creative experience to help you tell yours.

We are **mbaMission**, published authors with elite MBA experience who will work with you one-on-one to craft complete applications that will force the admissions committees to take notice. Benefit from straightforward guidance and personal mentorship as you define your unique attributes and reveal them to the admissions committees via a story only you can tell.

We will guide you through our "Complete Start to Finish Process":

- ☑ Candidate assessment, application strategy and program selection
- ☑ Brainstorming and selection of essay topics
- ☑ Outlining and essay structuring
- ☑ Unlimited essay editing
- ☑ Letter of recommendation advice
- ☑ Resume construction and review
- ☑ Interview preparation, mock interviews and feedback
- ☑ Post-acceptance and scholarship counseling

Monday Morning Essay Tip: Overrepresenting Your Overrepresentation

Many in the MBA application pool—particularly male investment bankers—worry that they are overrepresented. While you cannot change your work history, you can change the way you introduce yourself to admissions committees. Consider the following examples:

Example 1: "As an investment banking analyst at Bank of America, I am responsible for creating Excel models…."
Example 2: "At 5:30 pm, I could rest easy. The deadline for all other offers had passed. At that point, I knew…."

In the first example, the candidate starts off by mistakenly introducing the reader to the very over-representation that he/she should be trying to avoid emphasizing. In the second example, the banker immerses the reader in an unraveling mystery. This keeps the reader intrigued and focused on the applicant's story and actions rather than making the specific job title and responsibilities the center of the text. While each applicant's personal situation is different, every candidate can approach his/her story so as to mitigate the effects of overrepresentation.

To schedule a free consultation and read more than fifty Monday Morning Essay Tips, please visit our website:

www.mbamission.com